THE GREAT
AWAKENING

Volume - V

A series of superbly informative and prophetic messages, downloaded and transcribed originally as newsletters by

Sister Thedra

These precious messages are reprinted herein.

ISBN: 978-1-7363418-3-4

Contents

Mission Statement iv

THE TEMPLE OF SANANDA & SANAT KUMARA 1

TRANSCRIPTS OF THE MASTERS 104

Mission Statement

Give the truth to the world. Let it be received where it will. Many will read the messages. Some will accept the truth, others will read through curiosity, a few will ridicule. Yet to all is the truth given, and to all remains the power of choice.

The hope of the world in these times is in spiritualizing all forms of activity---promoting understanding through love and service. These must be the watchwords if the world is to come into lasting peace. We are trying to influence a world that is going astray and could cause undreamed of suffering. We are trying to overcome the thought of materialists and to bring a spiritual outlook into the earthly life. We need the help of all on earth who can think in spiritual terms. The great battle to be fought now is between the spiritual and the material, between idealism and carnalism. You can help by spreading the word---we are asking that you help because the battle may be long and the victory far away.

Halls of Light is not allied with any sect, denomination, political entity, organization, neither endorses nor opposes any cause. There are no dues for membership. Halls of Light is self-supporting through its own voluntary contributions. Halls of Light has but one purpose: to help through encouragement and understanding...

To contact the publishers or to obtain copies of our other books, please contact us at email: goldtown11@gmail.com

Esu Jesus Sananda

This reproduction is from an actual photograph taken on June 1st, 1961, in Chichen Itza, Yucatan, by one of thirty archaeologists working in the area at the time. Sananda appeared in visible, tangible body and permitted His photograph to be taken.

THE TEMPLE OF SANANDA & SANAT KUMARA

At the time Sister Thedra made her covenant with the Father that she would do His Will, she dedicated her life and will completely to the great assignment given to her by Sananda: "Go feed My Sheep". She learned to have absolute faith and confidence in His guidance and protection. She yielded her will completely to the Father, that His Will might be done "In her, thru her, by her and for her". She learned to live one day at a time, accepting all the trials and experiences of that day as part of her training for "The greater Part".

She sought to accept and "drain her cup of experience to the very dregs". Her sojourn in the High Andes was part of that training. She fully expected to spend the remainder of her life in the flesh in that region. It was eventually revealed to her that she would be sent back to her native land to carry out a mission that would be revealed to her at the proper time. She humbly accepted this assignment. At the expiration of five years, she was told that great responsibility would be placed upon her shoulders. She was to return to her native land and disseminate the Teachings of "The School of the Seven Rays" that she had and would continue to receive. She was sent back to California in 1961. not knowing how nor where she was to go or do. She relied on day to day instructions and guidance by her Teachers in the Higher Realms.

She lived in southern California for nearly a year, receiving daily instructions and revelations, which she shared with those who sought her counseling. In 1962 Sister Thedra was instructed by Sananda to go to Mt. Shasta to establish "His Work". She followed His instructions, and after coming to Mt. Shasta she again went thru many almost unbelievable trials, testings and betrayals at the hands of those who professed to be her friends who had volunteered to assist her in the work. Thru all of these trials, privations and disappointments, her steel will never wavered. She had complete faith in the continual assurance of Sananda that He knew exactly what was going on, and He "would be with her all the way". The instructions from both Sananda and Sanat Kumara for setting up the "Altar", "Temple" and "Gate House" are contained in the "Holy Scripts" that follow this "Portion".

After several moves here in Mt. Shasta, the present property was acquired in a most wonderful manner in 1965. The two Great Ascended Beings - Sananda and Sanat Kumara, who supervised the acquiring of the property, gave instructions that the Work should bear their Names. The work consists of both exoteric and esoteric aspects. The "Gate House" is the exoteric headquarters of the "Association Sananda & Sanat Kumara". The esoteric aspect is "The Temple of Sananda & Sanat Kumara".

Sister Thedra is the "Custodian or the Gate House" and "Priestess in the Temple". She has accepted the great responsibility of this assignment. She disclaims any special wisdom or other qualities that have led to the successful establishment of the Gate House and the wonderful activity carried on herein, and gives full credit to Sananda, Sanat Kumara and the Great and Mighty Council, who have not only provided the place and facilities; They are also providing the opportunity to sincere students to become "Associates" in this great Work of service to mankind. The activities of the Gate House are supported solely by the contributions of our associates. The complete story of the most remarkable career of Sister Thedra will become known in time to come. A.S.S.K

Christmas – 1974

Sori Sori -- Be ye as Mine hand made manifest unto them - say unto them as I would, that there shall be peace when they have given unto Me their hearts, their hands, their whole self - they shall then know peace, for it shall be established within them.

They shall have no hatred or animosity within them, for it is the way of the transgressor to be tormented by the hatred and hypocrisy - while the initiate finds peace within himself, for he is given unto peace.

Therefore I say unto them which cry: "Peace - Peace - Peace": First establish it within thine own self, and let others profit thereby. While I say unto ALL: "PEACE"- they have not partaken of Mine Peace, for they know Me not.

They have found not peace within their churches - their temples - their places of learning; neither have they turned unto their Source for Peace. They have been found in the "Places of worship" crying long and loud for so-called "peace", yet it hast availed them naught, for they have looked unto man - they have sought out their "Wise men" and consulted their oracles, and for that do I see them as ones defeated/ confused - running hither and yon as ones bewildered - while I stand before them, crying out: "Come unto Me and know ye Peace as I know; for I am the Lord of Hosts, sent of Mine Father that there be Peace established within them. I see them as bound in darkness, knowing not that I am come, even as the thief in the night.

3

I have said: 'Wait ye no more! come ye out from among them and follow where I lead thee, that ye might go where I go".

So be it that I am come to deliver out them which seek Me out - which hunger for the Light which I AM.

Fashion no gods for thyself; ask not of man - make ye no images of Me, for I am the Lord thy God! I am not bound by thine imagings - thine preconceived ideas or opinions of Me. I am the Risen Lord, the Lord of Lords, come that ye might know the true from the false - and I say there are false gods which would mislead the unwise - the mistaken - the ones bound by the father of lies, for he carefully lays his traps to mislead and misguide them which are unaware of his schemes.

I say his nefarious schemes have fallen on the fertile soil of them which seek signs and wonders - them which lay themself at his feet and ask for miracles; for he can and does show them marvels and signs - yet wherein has he freed them from bondage? He holds them bound in the places wherein they do languish, and cry out for Mine assistance. These are the ones which have followed him into the pit wherein he forsakes them - for he cares not for them after they have served his purpose.

I say he, the father of lies forsakes them and leaves them to languish in the pit. So be it ye shall do well to turn from him ere it is too late. I am thoughtful of thee, even in the time of thine torment and anguish. I say unto thee which follow Me, I am mindful of thee - even into the pit I reach out in Love and Mercy that they be delivered. So be it wise to hear ye Me, that ye be spared the fate of the traitors - for there are none so sad.

4

Let it be well with thee. when that hour comes that ye are called to go forth into the place of abode wherein ye shall be within thine new environment. I say the day swiftly approaches when thy name shall be called, and ye shall answer - let it be well with thee. Let it not be said, thou hast not heard Me, for I have called out unto thee: "Arise! Come ye out and be ye made whole".

I give Mine Peace unto all which hear Mine Voice and respond unto it. So let it be for all which have ears to hear, and a will to go where I go, for

I Am the Lord thy God

Recorded by Sister Thedra

Know Peace

Sori Sori -- For this hour let it be understood that there is much to do before they know Peace, for Peace comes not from their councils; their meetings shall fail to bring the peace which evades their efforts for they seek not PEACE - they seek power unto themself, each in his own way. They which cry for peace have not peace - for they ask for compromise, giving not of themself in PEACE.

The peace which they find shall be but the cessation of arms for a time, yet no peace shall come unto the lands of the Earth until they cleanse themself from all hatred, greed and malice - for within themself shall peace first be established.

Look not to any man for Peace; let it be born within thine own heart; therein is the beginning and the end. Let no man take from thee thy peace, for unto each it is given - he has but to accept it as

5

his heritage. PEACE is the LOVE OF GOD which shall <u>first</u> be established within each and every man.

The PEACE which I bring is within every man's reach. I say: Each and every man can attain such PEACE as I know, when he has accepted the fellowman, as I have accepted <u>him</u>; for the LIGHT of the WORD hast been given unto each, that he might abide upon the Earth with all other of his species.

The way is now open unto him, that he might come to know the plan for which he came into the world of form; form he hast, life he hast, yet he knows not his Source, neither his end - his destination. He wanders aimlessly, and for the most part arrogantly; he thinks of himself as <u>wise</u>, condemning all others unlike himself. For that does he falter and stumble, for none are like unto the other; for that reason do they take upon themself the responsibility of "self", that they might be as the Father would have them be. They go out as one in HIM, from HIM, and of HIM, yet separate from each other individually - that they be as "<u>ONE</u>" <u>in</u> <u>the</u> <u>species</u> <u>of</u> <u>man</u>, yet they are different in word and deed.

The WORD hast given unto each that cometh into the world a talisman that he carries with him, which no other can know, <u>until</u> his days upon Earth are finished, <u>then</u> they shall see and know even as I know, for all the masks shall at last be given up and be of no more account - they shall be NO MORE!

There shall be a coming together as "ONE" in whose company I shall stand and speak the Word: "<u>PASS</u> <u>YE</u>, <u>for</u> <u>thou</u> <u>hast</u> OVERCOME". The flesh shall no longer bind him who shall overcome.

6

I say: "The one which overcomes flesh shall be as a FREE SOUL, no longer bound in flesh - he shall run and weary not! he shall leap for joy and fall not! He shall sing a glad anthem and know that joy which shall be as the HOSTS', for the HOST shall take up the anthem and it shall ring out thru the Cosmos, praising the Name of SOLEN AUM SOLEN".

Recorded by Sister Thedra

Nov. 9, 1973

Now I Come Declaring

Sori Sori -- by Mine Grace shall ye be given that which shall profit thee -- ye shall first seek the LIGHT and ye shall not be deceived. Ye shall be as one responsible for the Word which is given unto thee thru this Mine handmaiden, for she hast proven herself trustworth - - and I find her trustworth in all things.

Be ye aware of Mine Word which is given unto thee thru and by this manner for it is good and I have declared it so -- so be it. Let thine tongue be swift to bear witness of Me, Mine word and Mine servant for I have claimed the Word, the Work perfect, so be it and Selah. I say ye shall find no fault with the method in which it is given, for it is given in such a manner that it shall profit thee to accept it.

I say: HOLY IS THE WORD -- and I declare it so! Be ye blest to receive it, for this I give it unto thee.

Now I come declaring unto thee this day, that I have raised up one which I have given the power and the authority to speak for me

7

-- I have given her Mine name that ye might have the knowledge which hast been kept for this day -- while I say there shall come ones declaring that they are mine anointed ones with the authority to speak Mine words -- I say that I know who is who -- and what is what! I say many are called and few are chosen -- this one I have called -- this one I have chosen.

I have chosen her for her capacity to learn of Me -- I have chosen her for her desire to follow Me. I have chosen her for her willingness to follow Me -- there is not any deceit within her -- there is no envy or malice within her -- yet, I say into her: "COME UP HIGHER FOR I HAVE GREATER THINGS IN STORE FOR THEE". She goes where sent and comes when called.

I have placed upon her head Mine hand and I have blest her, and she hast responded unto Mine touch -- she hast rested not on her laurels. She hast wasted not her talent which I have given unto her at the altar of the Lord thy God.

I say unto thee: hear ye Me and ye shall NOT put words into Mine mouth -- neither shall ye pilfer Mine words. Ye shall not deny Mine servant -- for to deny her is to deny Me. So be it I see them cry out against Mine servant while they claim to be following Me! I say unto them: "THOU HAST NOT SEEN ME, NEITHER HEARD ME".

I am come that they might know the true from the false, so let them see the LIGHT which I AM, and I say unto thee: I shall shew Mineself unto them which do seek the Light and come unto Me as a little child, clean of hand and heart.

Put thine hand in mine and I shall lead thee. Come and we shall walk together and rejoice for our communication, so be it as the Father would have it. Amen and Amen.

Recorded by Sister Thedra

Forewarning
April 24, 1974

Sori Sori -- For this day let Us consider the time which is upon us (now come) . It is for this that We, the Mighty Council find it expedient to speak unto thee, as thine Sibors, Counselors and Brothers. I say: The time is now come, when there shall be great upheaval, and great commotion - for the Earth too is going thru great changes, which shall bring much devastation and sorrow. Many shall go into the unknown realms unprepared, and they shall be confused, and sorrow shall fill them - I say: They shall sorrow, for they shall be as the ones unprepared.

Now the time is upon them, when they shall be brot out of the places wherein they have labored for bread, and they shall be as ones which have no hands - no feet with which to labor; they shall talk without sound, for they shall be as ones without physical tongue.

They shall speak., yet no sound shall be heard; they shall cry without tears - pity are they which go out unprepared. For this do We say: "Pay ye heed unto that which is said unto thee". - We speak that ye be prepared. Forget not that which is said, for We are not given unto idle speaking. Listen, Oh ye people! for it is for thy sake that We speak into thee! So let it profit thee to hear what is said.

9

April 21, 1974

Sori Sori -- Blest are they which come unto this Altar; Blest are they which hear that which I say; Blest are they which accept the Word, for I shall bless them as they have not been blest. Let them come - let them go - and they shall find that I am the One responsible for the Word which I give unto thee for them. Put thine hand in Mine, and I shall lead thee all the way. So be it ye shall not fail.

April 25, 1974

Sori Sori -- Place thine hand in Mine and I shall lead thee into greater heights, greater glories - and greater joys - so be it Amen.

May 1, 1974

Sori Sori -- For this day, let Us be as the Ones Sent that they might know that there are Ones which KNOW from whence. they come, and whereto they shall go. And let them learn that there are ones which have taken upon themself flesh and bone - born of woman - which still sleep - yet to awaken.

And these We, of the "Host" are to find and awaken; it is for their sake that We come into the Earth at this time. It is said: "They" shall awaken, and know that they have slept - slept overtime. Now they shall be found and awaken, and come forth as ones prepared to go all the way with Me the Lord thy God - so let it be and Selah.

Recorded by Sister Thedra

Things the Reader Should Know

Part - I

1. WHY DOES GOD THE FATHER, SANANDA, HIS SON, AND ALL OF THE OTHER SIBORS AND MESSENGERS FROM THE HIGHER REALMS, SPEAK AS ONE MAN: AS THOUGH ONE SINGLE PERSON WERE SPEAKING ALL TIME?

There is no other evidence of divinity in the revelations, writings and Temple teachings, "Recorded by Thedra," or any of the other divinely authorized 'channels," through whom those great revelations and recordings are coming - than the fact that all these writings are coming through one Divine Mind, The Apostle Paul said: "Let that mind be in you, which is in Christ Jesus." There is only one mind in all the worlds of the Gods; and that is the Holy Ghost Mind.

Present mankind is manifold diversification; to each his own individuality, everyone different from every other, In God's world, ONENESS is THE way of life. There is ONE, all -wise and true God; ONE Sananda; ONE Holy Ghost. Certainly attainment of Godhood includes the attainment of the ONE mind. Each individual Sibor therefore would speak with the same "tongue of an Angel."

Anyone who mistakenly criticizes or "finds fault" with this important ONENESS of style, merely betrays his or her lack of understanding of the ways of Godliness. In this world we are used to individuality and we expect, when uninformed about the Kingdom of God, to find divergence among the Angels. But one of the surest signs of divinity, is that every Angel of the Higher Rooms, will speak as ono man, ONE MIND, - God mind!

One of the surest ways to detect Astral, Nether World, psychic, mediumship communication, is that it will have divergence of style and the language will not be in the "tongue of an Angel." Mediumship, "spiritualism," will inevitably produce language which will sound like men of earth speaking. The Angelic manner of speaking will inevitable have a certain, easily detectable, (after much experience,) style. All channels, connected with Thedra, have this mark of divinity; the Sibors, the Sons of God who reveal Themselves to men of Earth, all speak as though they possess ONE MIND. Therefore, if one mindedness is not present - Beware, you are dealing with the dreaded Astral World.

2. IS THERE TOO MUCH REPETITION IN THE SIBOR'S TEACHINGS?

Any teacher of typing, shorthand, musical instruments or the use of any kind of machinery will readily agree to the necessity of arduous repetition, practice, and methodical over and over - overism. Concert pianists and violinists, for instance, will play one measure over and over literally thousands of times. (This writer was a piano teacher for forty-two years and speaks with Authority.)

A wonderful Biblical quotation, in the form of prophecy, says that in the last days "God will write His Law in their hearts! "Our hearts," our conscious minds, subconscious and super-conscious selves are what must be changed into the image of God, along with becoming physically, mentally, morally, culturally, socially, economically, and spiritually recreated, reformed, regenerated, transmuted and transformed into the image of God.

This "being born again," is a grand process. Sananda and all of the Sibors tell us that this process is to be accomplished by obedience to the words, principles and laws contained in the scripts. These teachers of the Higher Realms, being infinitely greater than any teachers of Earth, are infinitely more aware of the necessity of repetitions.

It is the tendency of people to read the same sentence or word such as "prepare," or "There are none so foolish as they who think themself wise," literally hundreds of times and never realize that they should be applying these statements to themselves. It is vey common practice while reading these "repetitous remarks", to think how they apply to "other people." As we read the repetitious phrases, we think how they apply to "Joe", "Mary" or "Ed" but often times, about the 439th time we read them, we begin to ask ourselves, "could this mean me?" "could it be possible that this applies to ME?" and then we begin to get the intended message.

People will road the phrase, "as you are prepared," many hundreds of times, and often complain about its repetitions - yet they don't got the idea, and the "message," that in order to get up to the place where Angels teach them, as promised, how to walk the "Royal Road," as Sananda and all of the other Angels have done, we must obey the laws and teachings and satisfactoriily pass the necessary training programs, initiations and disciplines along the way. People even foolishly scoff at the repetition instead of realizing how badly they need it. "Biting the hand that feeds them."

People who read these wonderful writings should ponder and think over the great sacrifices of these Divine Beings who have left their homes in Glory that we might be "gathered out from among them," that we might "be prepared", to be able to gain eternal life. Those words of these Sibors that appear repetitious, we should treat with great respect.

3. THESE VARIOUS SIBORS ARE INTRODUCING THEMSELVES AND THEY ARE BEING INTRODUCED FOR AN IMPORTANT PURPOSE.

It is quite necessary that the reader acquaint himself or herself with the names of those Sibors. You will soon be meeting these Holy Beings, - "when you are prepared," because each one will have charge of a certain part of Divine Knowledge - to add to the former - as you progress up the assembly line" toward final attainment.

This is the day of the Lord. This is the day or redemption, salvation and freedom from bondage. This is the foretold great day of enlightenment and illumination. This is the "day for which we have waited," when men and women, boys and girls are to "walk and talk with Angels as brothers and sisters. Jesus of Nazareth is back - "in flesh and bone," as He promised He would be, to give us out "inheritance," and prepare us for the place "wherein He is," in the place "He has prepared for us." Of course naturally, we must, as He taught, before "forsake the world and save our souls." These Holy Angels are now coming to tell us how. These scripts prepare us, by revealing the methods and laws of thought, speech, silence, behaviorism, attitudes, and whole heartedness for God; the necessary obedience to which prepares us for the ministration of

Angels. These Sibor Portions and the Temple Scripts are stepping stones into the Kingdom or God's Glory.

4. THESE ARTICLES, SIBORS PORTIONS, DIVINE EXPLANATIONS CLARIFICATIONS, TEMPLE TEACHINGS, AND REVELATIONS SHOULD BE GIVEN DUE AND PROPER RESPECT: THE SHOULD BE REVERED, CAREFULLY FILED AND KEPT IN THEIR PROPER ORDER OF SEQUENCE.

The reader should provide himself or herself with several 8 ½ x 11, three-hole looseleaf ring-book binders: for Sibors Portions, for articles from this Association, for Temple Teachings from this "altar." (The reader should expect to provide several looseleaf binders for Temple teachings alone) There are already hundreds of them and there are several being added each day.

The good that the reader will derive from these periodic receivals will largely depend on the respect, and reverence in which they are valued, and regarded by you.

Please help us, in this very important way. We like to hear from you from time to time. Open your heart. If for any reason these writings are not being read, respected, believed in or duly regarded, please write and tell us so. This request, we make sincerely and we will appreciate your cooperation.

We of course, know that the things of God are not for everybody.

5. WHAT SHOULD YOU DO REGARDING QUESTIONS THAT ARISE IN YOUR MIND AS YOU READ AND PONDER THESE WRITINGS?

Try to see this question from our viewpoint. It would take a vast "question and answer department" to begin to answer questions that come in from all points of the compass. God has not provided, nor do we think He will furnish funds for this purpose.

If the reader will just be patient - please? Later scripts, teachings, articles, and explanations - to follow - will adequately answer your earlier questions. As you read, and ponder, try to reason out the answers to your questions: write them down. As the answers come in later scripts, cross out the questions. This will be an interesting game to play, and it will be good for you.

6. PLEASE REMEMBER WE ARE NOT CONDUCTING A "FORTUNE-TELLING BOOTH."

Because Sister Thedra and others, here are receiving Divine Revelations from God and Holy Angels, pertaining to the Kingdom Of God, some people get the idea that this os a "Dear Abby" or "Ann Landers" type of Human Relations and counseling Service. Some go so far as to ask Sister Thedra the kind of questions one would expect from a "Fortune Teller." Some write and ask whether they are going to marry a blonde or brunette, if and when they are going to rent their house or sell their property, etc. Those kind of questions, naturally are quite removed from eternal questions of salvation. One lady sent Thedra a lock of her hair, and wanted to know if her baby's hair would be the same color.

Then again you have the kind of person who will want to show off his or her personal wisdom by learning some future event so that after it come to pass, this person can appear like a prophet. There are many motivations for asking questions. They are legion. Of course, such antics can only result in being ignored completely. This Association feels that it has a sacred responsibility which is that or preparing those who want such preparation to meet and by instructed by Divine Beings - to gain ascendency over the woes disappointments, frustrations, transient pleasures and imitation joys of this world. It is our task to help people overcome "The wheel of rebirth."

7. STUDY, PONDER, READ AND REREAD THESE WRITINGS.

In order for the reader to derive the intended benefit from these messages it will be necessary and advisable to study them, meditate upon them, and search them. "Once over lightly," is little better than nothing. These articles will, when properly treated, envelop the reader in a protective atmosphere of Godly influence. They will clothe him in the kind of vibrations conducive to Godly living.

Sananda tells us plainly that believing in and keeping sacred these writings will inevitably cause us to obey them, if they are properly respected. In the articles to follow in this same series much more light will be shed on this subject.

8. WHY THE GRAMMATICAL ERRORS AND MIS-SPELLED WORDS?

This is the day when the "wisdom of the wise is to perish." Man's education and learning have been played up; God's kind of learning and knowledge is now being played down. People have false standards of measurements. Sananda has deliberately ordained that people of "critical eye" be tripped up. The thought, intended meaning, subject matter is what these writings are meant to convey. These articles and other writings from this Association will show the reader that we know the difference between good and bad grammar and between correct and incorrect spelling, punctuation and composition. If a reader is the kind of person who looks for faults instead of truth, accuracy instead of sense, then he or she will find plenty of rope with which to spiritually hang himself or herself.

Divine Explanations

Part - 2

The White Brotherhood and the Emerald Cross

THE MANY QUESTIONS ABOUT THE WHITE BROTHERHOOD AND THE ORDER OF THE EMERALO CROSS MAY BE EXPLAINED IN A FEW SIMPLE WORDS.

ONE HAS TO EARN THE RIGHT TO BECOME A MEMBER -- - EITHER IN THIS LIFE OR OTHERS BEFORE OR AFTER--- NONE ENTER UNPREPARED.

THE WHITE BROTHERHOOD - or - THE ROYAL ASSEMBLY - is of the Realms of Light---not of Earth. The ascended Masters have proven themself in the school of Earth (THE SCHOOL FOR GODS) who have trodden the path of INITIATION - Overcome the trials and temptations of the mundane world - who have gained their freedom and ascended as the Lord Jesus Christ (Sananda). They have gone the ROYAL ROAD.

Knowing the path of the Initiate -- and its pitfalls -- and sorrow, they extend a hand in Fellowship - LOVE and WISDOM - NEVER

18

depriving the candidate an opportunity to learn his lessons well -- for this is His salvation -- for this do they proffer their hand, NOT to do our part for us, but rather that we become strong and free by our own strength. The Royal Assembly or the White Brotherhood have known all of the heart aches, the longing, crucifications, temptations and JOYS of the aspirant -- the candidate -- the Master -- the Sibor -- herein lies their strength, their understanding, their great love for us on the path. Their love and understanding knows no bounds. They give help when necessary for our progress. They also withhold it wisely - should it deprive us of our lessons.

The candidate on the path of initiation shall become self-responsible for all his actions -- all the energy allotted him throughout his whole EARTHLY existence - and take atonement for all his misused energy - for therein is his salvation. There is no one else which will ever make this atonement for us (the candidate) on the path of unfoldment. While the most of "WHITE BROTHERS" Brothers or LIGHT are ready to assist, the candidate shall (MUST) put forth every effort to overcome all the forces of darkness which would dater his progress and earn for himself his freedom from BONDAGE,

The Emerald Cross

THE EMERALD CROSS - is a company - and order of beings, who work within the Brotherhood OF MAN - and the Fatherhood of God - For the good of all mankind ---- And at the head of this group one known as MOTHER SARAH, the personification of love -- embodiment of all MOTHERS. That is: the LOVE of God made manifest - in MOTHERS. The blessed Mother Sarah is the head of this Order of the Emerald Cross.

And when one earns the Divine right and privileges to associate themself with this Order, it is the joy of all the Orders - and Brothers of Light. I speak for the Order - for I am known as Merseda.

As told to Sister Thedra of the Order of the Emerald Cross.

CONANCHE - which is the porter at the door - which both keep out the unworthy, the unjust, the unclean. The Door Keeper - the one responsible for the Temple Gate.

BITTER CUP - that which you would not like to partake of - that which poisons thee - that which is not good - that which torments thee - that which ye have given unto thy brother to torment hint - which returns unto thee as a boomerang to torment thee - which ye shall receive multiplied -- which has accumulated in its swift flight. I say prepare not for thyself the bitter cup for ye shall drink of the portion which thou doth prepare for thy brother. Be ye not foolish - make it not bitter.

BLEST OF MINE BEING - I have given of Mine self that Mine beloved has being.

BLEST OF MINE PRESENCE - Have I not gone the long way. I have gone out from Mine place of abode that I might bring light unto the Earth that she might be lifted up - that the children thereof might be delivered of all bondage - that they might return unto the place from whence they went out. And have I not come unto thee many times that this be accomplished? Have I not done all which has been given unto me to do? Wherein have I failed thee? have I not done all that I have come to do? - While it is not as yet finished, I shall not fail. Mv mission shall be finished ere I return unto Mine abiding place. Shall I not be unto thee true and shall I not return the Victor?

GAVE OF HIMSELF - Did I not give of Mine Self - hast thou? Have I not been true unto Mine trust? Have I asked aught FOI Myself? Have I not done that which I have promised? Have I not given Mine All? Have I not come on a sacrificial Mission? What more have I to give - Other than myself.

PORE - The physical body - vehicle which thou dost use.

INITIATION - Thy preparation for the inner temple. Each step is an initiations. One step at a time - the overcoming of self - the world - the becoming that which I am.

COSMOS - That which is unseen throughout many universes by thy eyes. Great is the expanse of the Father's Kingdom and the total thereof is referred to as "throughout the Cosmos."

LORD'S STRANGE ACT - This I shall reveal in Mine own time.

WALK WHICH WAY THY CROWN TILTS NOT - as a Son of God. Do honor unto try Father Mother God - and thou shall be as one which has the Royal Raiment upon thine shoulders - and ye shall wear it in honor and with dignity.

WHEN IT SAYS IT IS RECORDED - WHEREIN IS IT RECORDED? - In the secret place - in the ether - and within the inner temple - and wherein thou art are many things recorded - which I do speak of. Ye shall see these recordings when thru doth enter into the secret place of Mine abode. I say ye shall read the records wherein are written the records of all thy travels from the time ye left the Father Mother God until thine return unto Him.

WHAT IS MICHAEL'S FLAMING SWORD? - "The "Sword of Truth and Justice."

Recorded by Sister Thedra:

Part - 2

9. WHAT YOU SHOULD DO ABOUT THE VARIOUS SLIPS.

When you receive things from this office, unless it is a completed article or one without parts, it may have a colored slip on the last page. The color of these slips is a code to us - different colors for different articles or clarifications. In order to receive the continuation of a particular article or section or part, it is necessary that we have you send in these colored slips. In this way we know what you have read.

Your interest, enthusiasm, desire for more, reaction after reading and the extent of your desire for the next portion or part all have a definite effect on what, when, and how much we mail to you at one time. We like to hear from you, from time to time. If you want material to come faster, send in your colored slips, even before you read what you have received. Depending upon where you live from Mt. Shasta, California, it will take a prescribed time to get back an answer, so, send your colored slips as soon as you get them, and this will give you an opportunity to "digest" each receival before the next one arrives, and at the same time you will be paving the way for sooner getting the next part.

10. MORE ABOUT HOW TO STUDY, PONDER, READ AND REREAD.

Each sentence in the Holy words of the Angels should be read slowly, deliberately, and carefully. Each phrase should be weighed and pondered. The thoughts conveyed, what the words mean, the intended "message" should be considered and thoroughly understood.

Tremendous promises are contained in these writings. What could be more wonderful than a life of Heavenly joy---forever? Think what it would mean to be a partaker of God's greatest gift of Eternal Life! Behold how marvelous to attain unto oneness with the Father and receive your inheritance in full. This is what is promised us if we will learn what is in these Scripts and obey the conditions set forth. This will, of course, depend on comprehension and this will be proportionate to how thoroughly we study, ponder, read and reread. Sananda says: "We must dive deep for His pearls."

11. PLEASE DO NOT LOAN YOUR MATERIAL TO OTHERS.

There are various reasons why people loan their reading material to others: friends, and associates, etc. --- they think, often-times this will help us. There is a much better way. Each person who wants benefit from learning about and being helped by the Sibors, Temple Scripts and articles from this "Altar" should definitely, permanently, and quickly get in touch with this office and procure all of this information for himself or herself.

In the first place you, dear Reader, should have at your instant Command, in your own possession, all material up to date for reference and rereading, for correlating and rechecking purposes. You cannot do this if part of it is over at Joe's house or over at your sister Mary's place. It should be carefully filed and systemically bound at your place. Show your books most surely: but encourage and insist that others get in touch with us themselves. This is the way to help Sananda and this is the way to help us.

The counsel, teachings, admonitions, suggestions and advice contained in these revelations and clarifications is for you. Many readers can see how they better apply to someone else -- but they are meant for you. This is one of the most difficult things we are trying to get people to see that you are the one to whom these Sibors are speaking. They are not meant for Joe or Frank, or Clarice, liner Sananda says "they" or "them" to Sister Thedra --- He means "you." It is wonderful to realize that you are to take it to "them," but the teachings in them are also for "you!"

12. HOW IS THIS IMPORTANT WORK FINANCED?

Although we have been instructed by Sananda that this be done with no price tags or commercial considerations attached to this work --- so that no undue hardships be placed on anyone who cannot pay at all, or on them who can pay but little --- at the same time, Sananda is quite specific in His instructions that people will be blessed in their efforts, assistance and helpfulness with this work.

It does take money from donations, contributions, tithes and offerings to bring this knowledge to the attention of people.

The outlay from this office in expenses from paper, mimeograph ink and stencils, postage and incidental expenses is considerable.

Therefore, we do appreciate and need financial help. Neither Thedra nor anyone else connected with this office receive any salary or financial benefit from this endeavor. Every one of us is wholly dedicated and one-hundred percent consecrated to God the Father, Sananda and all of the Sibors, We are on call twenty-four hours a day. Every waking moment is devoted exclusively to the work of God. Every hour, sixteen to eighteen a day, seven days a week, including so-called holidays, are spent in wholehearted joyful surrender to this effort.

Our needs are ever expanding. We know the readers are blessed (and we are grateful for this,) when they assist in this work. We are prepared and authorized to promise that you will be blessed when you contribute to this cause. No one is to be asked for money. This we leave to you and the prompting of the spirit.

13. THERE IS MUCH TO COME FROM THIS "ALTAR," OFFICE AND ASSOCIATION.

The reader should be prepared for much to come from this source of light. In addition to the Sibors Portions consisting of 201 pages, there are hundreds of Temple teachings up to this date and they are being received from time to time, and many articles, instructions, explanations and writings of interest to the reader which will be sent as you are ready. While in South America, Thedra received many revelations which have been sealed up to come forth in the immediate future.

Therefore the reader is urged to follow through. This is the day of great revelation. The present work of the Angel Moroni and his coming into embodiment again is a tremendous subject with which everyone should keep abreast.

Sananda says that what has been revealed up to now is only the beginning. of "the work of the Father," Manifold preparations have been made and a great foundation has been laid for this culmination of events. This is the day for "the Lord's Strange Act." Therefore it will behoove the reader to let nothing interfere with his or her continuation of study and illumination from this "Association of Sananda Sanat Kumara."

14. IT IS NOW, AGAIN, A CASE OF "ALL OLD THINGS HAVE PASSED AWAY AND ALL THINGS HAVE BECOME NEW."

Sananda says, often, in recent revelations that now He is come, and through revelation is beginning to establish truth and light among men, preparatory to gathering out from "among them," His elect --- that we are no longer under the old law.

In the days when Jesus walked among the Jews, He warned that they should not try to put His new wine into their old bottles. He was opposed to their attempts at regarding His new teachings as a patch. to put on their old dilapidated garments.

Now, in these days, the situation is precisely the same. Our old, diversified, adulterated beliefs, thread-bare opinions, worn-out precepts, and false traditions, many of them inherited from our fathers, must give way to the new bright light, illuminating light and Godly light being ushered in, now, by Sananda and these Angelis messengers from the Higher Realms.

Men, educated by me, indoctrinated by men, who have learned only from men, well-meaning as they have been, have been teaching us what they have learned from men, about what other man have thought in regards to so-called truths, --- these are largely a hodge-podge from darkened minds of men which has all combined to make a wilderness of doctrines, dogmas and diatribes, which at present have nothing in common whatever with real truth. Man's present wisdom, the Sibors tell us, has no resemblance to the wisdom of God.

Therefore the reader must expect to constantly find, in these writings, that which is new and different from his old concepts and beliefs. These "legirons" will terribly bind the reader if he allows them to do so. Do not expect these Holy Angels to confirm or re-establish false doctrines or erroneous concepts. It is now a case of letting "all old things pass way," and accepting the realization that "all things should and must "become new!" We say, again - don't try to put this new wine in old bottles."

15. WHAT ARE THE PURPOSES AND OBJECTIVES OF THIS ASSOCIATION, BY WHOM WAS IT ESTABLISHED: AND WHY WAS IT ESTABLISHED AT MT. SHASTA, CALIFORNIA?

This association, consisting of wholly dedicated, one-hundred percent consecrated, completely devoted to God people: --- Temple and Altar of "Sananda, Sanat Kumara' was established for the following purposes and objectives: -

1. - For the purpose of acting as a channel through which Sananda, the "director" of the New Dispensation and Sanat Kumara, who is

27

in charge of the "Holy Mountain," as well as many other Sibors from the Higher Realms, may reveal the mind and will of God to the sons and daughters of Earth.

2. - For the purpose of becoming a Headquarters of dissemination and dispensing knowledge, information, instructions, messages, revelations, teachings, and intelligence about the plans, purposes, methods, and systems that God is now preparing to use to effect the rescue, salvation and redemption of the people of the Earth; those who desire freedom from earthly darkness, bondage and unhappiness; from coming catastrophes, woes, sorrows; tribulations, pestilences, famine, and judgements.

3. - With the objective that people who want to be saved from the natural effects of rebelliousness, ignorance, commandment breaking, lawlessness, hate, selfishness, hellishness, etc. of mankind --- may do so by obedience to the higher laws of the Christ Life as exemplified by Jesus and now re-established in the Holy scripts of God the Father, His son Sananda and all these Holy Angels.

4. - To act as a gathering place, a refuge focus point where men and women who wish to abandon the world and follow Sananda in all things, may live the necessary Holy life of obedience to Sananda -- - in order to learn how to "walk the Royal Road" into Eternal Life. Only those who obey these conditions have any assurance that they will escape the dreaded days ahead.

This "Association of Sananda and Sanat Kumara" was established by commandment and instruction from these two Sibors, personally.

Mt. Shasta is a Holy place, within this mountain are many Divine rooms, in which initiations, and Holy ordinances are given. Also, this mountain is strategically located. It is geographically safer than most locations.

Part - 3

16. ETERNAL WORDS - What is the meaning of this term?

A wonderful Letter Day Scripture foretells the coming of the "One Mighty and Strong," (Sananda, Jesus Christ, the Wayshower,) "whose mouth shall utter words, Eternal words," This phrase, "Eternal words," is of great significance. It is vital that each candidate or initiate along the path have a bless understanding of the meaning of this expression.

We, as finite individuals, with our limitations find it difficult to comprehend infinity. When God speaks, whether Solen Aum Solen, Sananda or any of the various Sibors, (who all speak as the One Divine Mind,) they express themselves from their standpoint of infinity. They do not seek according to man's finite understanding --- but rather in their infinite, timeless, spaceless infinity.

For Example: The Scripts contain the phrases "This Day:" --- This is My Day; "--- "This is the day for this to be accomplished," or "This is My Day for which I have waited;" ---"This is the day for which ye have long awaited."

We, in our finite concepts might mistakenly think that this could mean some particular Tuesday or Thursday. We might even think that it means some particular week or month, etc., but when we look at it in the meanings God wishes to convey from His point of view

29

--- attempting as best we can to see things in infinity, "This Day," means from now on, this whole "letter day," this last Dispensation, "The New Age," - "The Consummation of the Age," The Golden." Therefore the term "This Day" is not referring to a day of the week or a date of the month or year.

THE ETERNAL "NOW."

When we as man say "now," - we, of course, mean right now, today, this instant. But when infinity says "now," because with Deity all things are present, whether to us they are past, present or future -- everything is "now." To Deity "now" is always "present. " Since everything is always present, then everything is always now. "The Golden Present is Eternity Itself!"

Yes, to understand "Sibor language" we have to raise our sights." An "Eternal Word" is one which has an Eternal meaning; a word which is co-eternal with infinity,

Take the word "faith" for example. This is not something that we use as a stepping stone, something which passes away at some given point, faith, being co-eternal with God, continues Forever with God. Eternal life is a life of Eternal principles, Eternal attributes, Eternal Consideration, Eternal understandings and comprehensions.

Therefore, we us strive to learn to reason and think from the Sibor's vantage point, from their point of view. Our considerations must give way to their intended meanings. Our tiny, limited thinking must be raised in order to grasp "Eternal Words."

The next heading on becoming prepared will further illustrate the meaning of "Eternal" as it pertains to the word "prepare."

17. WHAT IT MEANS TO BECOME PREPARED. When, where and how is this preparation accomplished? These are, in all probability, the best important questions that it is possible for an initiate to ask.

In the beginning of this all-important discussion of the meaning of the word "prepare," we wish to begin by requesting Sananda's explanation of "preparation," as stated in "Divine Explanations," Part 1.

"What do you mean by "preparation"? "This my beloved is the part which they shall do - the part of preparation is: cleaning thyself of all thy opinions, indoctrinations of men. The cup must be emptied. This is thy part, the becoming the "little child" un-opinionated, unscathed and un-seer with or by their doctrines, creeds, and crafts. I say the child is un-indoctrinated and un-opinionated and is the virgin mind - (yet it does not remain so long in this world). While the little child represents the empty cup - the empty vessel, the Virgin Spirit, it is given unto the child to be one which has come from other realms and to have been in many embodiments, many times: yet the symbol of virginity. Wherein is it said there are none innocent among thee?"

Before discussing the "Eternal" aspects of this word "prepare," it would be good to point out what is suggested by the word itself. In view of the above quotation from Sananda's own words, the reader will find much food for thought in the following analysis

The word "pare" means to peel, uncover, like you pare a potato when it is peeled. To pre - pare, therefore, means to pre - peel.

31

In Ancient times "circumcision" was introduced to preclude this infinite principle. Jesus, in Maridian of Time, personally came to fulfill this Ancient Law, teaching that it was "a broken heart and a contrite spirit," that the Ancient law was instituted to symbolize. Circumcision typified the making, the paring or peeling down of this bodily organ possible as a signification of paring down or peeling the heart; this was to symbolize the uncovering or exposing the old heart to the light of the new truth.

As Sananda says, we all come into this world innocent but we can't stay that way long. As soon as we can learn, we begin to pick up the false tenants, false beliefs and doctrines of the world.

The reason this part of the body was used to demonstrate circumcision of heart is that, that is wherein and by which conception takes place. Becoming a little child must begin, naturally, with conception. Conception in a spiritual way begins with "circumcision of heart." The reader can understand that this is a subject of many ramifications.

Suffice it to say, as Paul the Apostle understood it, "neither circumcision nor uncircumcision availeth anything, but a new creature." This is the important thing, becoming a new creature.

Being reconceived by caring, peeling, uncovering our old, wrong, faulty, unreal precepts, false doctrines, preconceived ideas, false standards, false evaluations and the affections, desires, loves, ambitions, aspirations and vanities, etc. of the world --- and letting Sananda replace the old, in every direction, in every dimension, in every consideration --- with His new Eternal life principles, hopes, ideals and blessedness.

This reasoning gives new meaning to the word "prepare." It means, simply, "take off the old, put on the new."

The main consideration, therefore, in regards to this word "prepare" --- is to realize that it is an explanation of the old word "repent." The scriptures have said, many times, that "salvation, redemption depended on repentance." But we have never had a clear understanding of the meaning of the word "repent."

Now the Sibors are giving us a new word, "prepare." We find that it is more than just to cease from doing evil deeds, but that to prepare is to give up our faulty thinking, faulty ambitions, worldly learning, etc. end to begin anew, desiring instead --- Godliness, perfection, spiritual attainments and Holy comprehension.

When builders, (even in our world,) went to put a beautiful new building in place of an old dilapidated one, it is necessary to first tear down and get rid of the old structure. God is a master builder. He cannot be expected to be less wise than man.

Before God can give us Eternal life and make us fit company for the Angels to occupy Christ's "many Mansions" or Heaven, we must first be willing to "pare" or peel off our old thoughts, beliefs, loves and habits. We are a composite of our old habits, opinions and preconceived ideas.

One should carefully take stock, measure himself or herself and endeavor to ascertain where our old thoughts and ideas come from. We should constantly ask the question, was man the source of my knowledge or was God the author of my opinions?

WHEN, WHERE, AND HOW IS PREPARATION MADE ?

The word prepare, being an eternal word must be looked upon as a forever word. We will be eternally preparing for something higher. We have to first be about preparing to walk the "Royal Road" which is constantly preparing us for our inheritance in full which will, in turn, be preparing us to prepare others to be preparing for endless preparing. Each step of the way prepares us for the next step. Each initiation prepares us for the next.

We should see ourselves, eventually standing in the presence of the Father, being given our Sonship, and our Eternal Father saying to us "Now you are prepared to go on eternally preparing." It is like the universe, if you care to the end of it --- what should be on the other side? Therefore, powers is an Eternal word. Of course, it goes without saying that each step its trials, initiations, headaches, doubts, fears, etc. --- out with joy, added capacity for love and service. These are also Eternal words. There is an Eternal balance – "as ye give so shall ye receive," --- "as ye receive so shall ye give."

When, therefore, do we become prepared?

ETERNALLY! WHERE DO WE BECOME PREPARED?

Do we have to someplace to be alone somewhere, to become prepared? When Jesus was on earth, He used every situation, took advantage of every opportunity to practice and demonstrate the will of God. He steered every conversation into Godliness. He constantly worked at "His father's business," and He did it among people. Jesus was and is our example in all things.

34

Stay right where you are, at the moment, and begin immediately practicing on your friends. See how kind, thoughtful, cheerful, patient, gentle, tender, merciful, and full of love you can be. See how humble, selfless, sympathetic and understanding you can be. Meditate on perfection. Become filled with desire to absorb all of Sananda's teachings. Let Sananda's light shine in you and through you. You do not have to concern yourself for a moment; His infinity covers you every second you live. He knows what you are doing and what you are thinking all the time. When he wants you to do something special He'll get word to you. In the meantime, work for God right where you are.

HOW TO BECOME PREPARED ?

Like learning to play a violin, drive a car, make a dress, or master the typewriter --- it takes practice, ceaseless, constant, industrious practice. It takes wholehearted practice. It takes endless and constant reading of the Scripts. It takes much basking in the Eternal words of the Scripts. It will take appreciation, and gratitude to Solen Aum Solen as we should ceaselessly praise His Holy Name. We must give credit and credence to Sananda. But most of all, we become prepared first, last and always by obedience to Sananda.

HOW DO WE EMPTY OUR CUP ?

The method is simple, you simply start pouring in Eternal words. They force out the old. Sananda's words can be trusted. We may question them sometimes, but it is only our preconceived ideas that are at fault. Keep pouring in Eternal Words and the purifying, regenerating, Eternalizing process will be going on faithfully, oblivious to you. It takes time, it takes effort. Whatever you do, keep

35

in touch with this office, this Temple, this "Altar." This is the disseminating point for Solen Aum Solen, Our Father Mother God through Sananda.

Pour Out The Old Wine

Beloved – This day let it be recorded that which I say unto thee - that they might bear witness of these Mine Words -- I AM the LORD GOD -- I AM of MINE FATHER sent that there BE LIGHT within the world of Men -- There IS LIGHT -- I say: BEHOLD THE LIGHT WHICH I AM ---

Let it be known that I AM COME - and as they are prepared - so shall they receive of Me -- I say: They shall first prepare themselves for to receive ME - then - I shall reveal Mineself unto them---

Too I say: - Pity are they which deny Me - for poor in Spirit are they! ---

I say unto thee: Behold ME the LORD thy GOD - and Know ye that thou art Not Alone ---

I Am Come that there be Light - and no man shall keep Mine own from Me -- For I come that I might find Mine own -- And Mine "Flock" shall hear Mine Voice and answer Me ---

When I say unto them: "COME - follow ye Me" -- They shall lay down their implements of war - their pruning shears - and their titles/ their letters/ their degrees -- They shall throw off the yoke/their mantles/ their garments of State – And they shall follow

36

Me - as ones glad and joyous -- For the Peace which is Mine – is that which they have <u>not</u> <u>found</u> within their places of abode ---

I say: - They have <u>Not Known Peace</u> – for the Peace which I bring – no man can put asunder – nor take from thee ---

I say: Come – Follow ye Me – and I shall give unto thee Water More Potent Than OLD WINE --- Pour Out the thine "Old Wine" – And I shall give unto thee LIVING WATER ---

So let it be ---

I AM Sananda

Recorded by Sister Thedra of the Emerald Cross

Song of Sananda

Beloved Ones ---

Let this day bring forth Fruit –

Let this day bring forth Fruit –

Let this day bring forth Fruit –

Let this day bring forth Great Harvest –

Let this day bring forth Great Harvest –

Let this day bring forth Great Harvest –

Let this day be Glad --

Let this day be Glad --

Let this day be Glad --

Let this day bring an Onrush of Light --

Let this day bring an Onrush of Light --

Let this day bring an Onrush of Light --

Let this day bring a Great Onrush of Peace --

Let this day bring a Great Onrush of Peace --

Let this day bring a Great Onrush of Peace --

So be it and Selah --

Sananda

Recorded by Sister Thedra of the Emerald Cross

Capital Punishment

-- While it is but a short while until their Activities shall be ended –
I say it is now the beginning of the end --

There shall be Greater Stress before the end -- For ALL their
hatred - ALL their bigotry - ALL their weakness - shall confront
them -- They shall be as ones tormented by their own weakness -
their foolishness and their hatreds -- For is it not said: "That which
they send out shall return unto them - and it shall either bless or
torment them" ---

It is clearly written -- "That which they send forth shall return unto them - as bread upon the water" So shall they eat thereof -- And they shall be responsible for that which they have sent out -- It is not an <u>unjust</u> law - for it is the law which IS and ever shall BE -- So be it that no man shall set it aside - or make it void ---

Let it be said that they which bring forth the law of death - shall live by the law -- They shall be responsible for that which they bring forth -- They shall not place their responsibility upon another - that they escape the law -- Let it be Known that when one takes upon himself the responsibility of depriving another his right to express thru the form of flesh - he hast transgressed THE LAW - and he alone shall atone for it - <u>None Other!</u> -- Too - it shall be stated here - that the ones which stands witness - bear testimony of their actions - and raise NOT their voice in protest - are not innocent of GUILT - - They are likewise accountable for their past -- For I say - to uphold the law of JUSTICE is the part of ALL men which expect justice -- Now let it be understood --- NO MAN shall take the law into his own hands -- He shall <u>not</u> KILL -- This hast been said MANY TIMES! - in many ways - yet they make a mockery of the law -- And they spit upon the Words which have come forth from MINE OWN MOUTH! ---

I say they are willful - and they are to be found wanting!

So be it I shall again this day - give unto thee another part for them - which shall be added unto this -- So let it be -- I am with thee that they might know that which I say -- Let them take heed -- For I say - woe unto them which go headlong unto their downfall -- I say unto them: STOP! - LOOK! - SEE! - that which ye bring upon thine own self -- So be it I say unto thee Mine Beloved: - return again this day unto this Altar - and I shall speak unto them which are the errant ones ---

While it is time now for them to come forth and declare the Truth - and be as ones prepared - they shall be given that which is necessary for their preparation -- And they shall either <u>choose</u> it - or reject it -- Yet I say unto them - they prepare <u>themself</u> - none other -- <u>They</u> are responsible for their own preparation - and they shall find no "Scapegoat" which hast the power to do their preparation for them-- There is no such law - which shall make it possible ---

Now let it be said - that they which practice such injustice - one unto the other - as they are wont to do - shall be unprepared in that day - when they shall stand as ones shorn of ALL their power - ALL their vain glory -- and when they shall be caught up short of their course -- So be it that I have given of Mineself that they be prepared to go where I go -- Yet none enter into Mine Place of Abode unprepared -- So be it that I say AGAIN - prepare thineself - that ye might enter into the INNER TEMPLE with Me -- For this have I come - that ye be prepared -- So let it BE -- What else matters? So be it - I COME that THERE BE LIGHT -- THERE IS LIGHT –

See IT and walk ye therein ---

I AM the Lord thy God --

Sananda

Recorded by Sister Thedra of the Emerald Cross

40

Pilfer the Words of No Man

Beloved Ones -- This day I would give unto thee this Word -- And be it understood that ALL which ask for Light shall receive -- Now when it is come that ye have made thin self-ready for to receive of Me and by Me - I shall reveal Mineself unto thee -Ye need not Go into any place -- Ye need not ask of any man -- Neither shall ye bow down before any strange god - and ask of him favors ---

I say - ye shall have no need of thine idols - THINE portions - which have been unto thee sedatives/ sedations* -- Ye have said thine mantras - as rigamaroles -- and as poultices they have served thee ---

While it is now time to be up and about thine Fathers business - - Alert thineself and be self-responsible - responsible for thine own words/ deeds/ actions -- Pilfer the words of no man for they are his -- Make of thine own self a chalice - that it might be filled to overflowing - that others might fill themself from the overflow -- For there are ones which have a lesser capacity --

Fret not for them - for they are content with the droplets from the cascade - which abounds endlessly and without ceasing! ---

Wherein is it written - that I shall be the oil in thine lamp? -- I speak unto thee in parables - that ye might know that which is the law - that ye might come to Know ME as I AM ---

Now ye shall be as ones prepared to accept the fullness of ME - and I shall not deny thee - for MINE FATHER AND I ARE ONE - - Hear ye that which I say unto thee - MINE FATHER AND I ARE

41

ONE -- Be ye ONE with ME - and I shall lead thee out of BONDAGE!!

I AM that I AM -

Recorded by Sister Thedra of the Emerald Cross

* That which has lulled thee to sleep -

Mighty! Mighty! Is the Word of God!

Blest are they which receive IT unto themself -- And so shall it BE -- So shall they be blest of ME the LORD GOD - sent of Mine Father that THERE BE LIGHT -- So be it I AM HE Which cometh in the Night while they sleepeth - knowing not that "I AM COME"!

I say unto thee: - Declare unto them - I AM COME! ---

Wait upon ME and I shall show thee GREATER things than they have dreamed of -- I say unto them: AWAKEN that ye might SEE the GLORY of the LORD --

Yet they sleep -- They grovel for a pittance - and wage war upon one another -- They spit upon Mine Word - and call themself "Wise"---

Poor Foolish Mortals!

I say unto them "COME' - and they move not -- They have no fear of the darkness - yet they turn from the Light ---

I say - they are the ones which know not ---

I Am COME that they KNOW -- yet they shall turn from their wonton/willful way - and follow after Me ---

I come not to show Mine wounds - or perform for them MIRACLES - that they might follow Me ---

I GIVE of Mineself that they might KNOW the TRUTH - which shall free them from BONDAGE ---

I bring No Creed - nor Dogma ---

I COME SOLELY because of MINE LOVE for them ---

I AM the Lord thy God -

Sananda

Recorded by Sister Thedra of the Emerald Cross

Abortions
--Sananda

When it is come that they bring forth children which are malformed - and they deny them - and their right to express themself - they are as ones preparing for themself the 'bitter cup' -- For I say unto thee - the "Procreation act is Sacred" - and it shall not be given unto them to escape the law -- When they use it for their own satisfaction - without thot of the results thereof - I say unto them - they are responsible for the results thereof!

When they call forth A BEING - that he might take upon himself a vehicle of flesh - and then they destroy that embryonic vehicle - it is indeed their "bitter cup"-- For it shall bring about a race of

43

barren women - which hast not the power to bring forth - and the fortune to be tormented thereby! -- I say - they shall be tormented because of their inability to bring forth children -- These shall be as ones which have not heeded the law of procreation -- These shall be the ones which have given of themself in sexual indulgence - and self indulgence - without the Light which governs such creation.

Let it be said that there are none exempt of/or from the law -- The abortions are the undoing of many which are now practicing such - as they are wont to be free from responsibility -- While it is said that there are none exempt from the law - there are ones which are incapable of bringing forth offspring -- These are ones which have fortuned such conditions unto themselves in time past -- And they too are under the law -- Let it be said that they are not innocent of these things which hast brot about such results ---

Let it be said that they shall suffer the results of such as abortion - and they know not how great their suffering shall be ---

Such is Mine Word unto thee this day -- A Word should be sufficient - yet they shall go their way - and heed not that which I say ---

So be it that I see them as a heedless lot -- For this have I spoken out - that they which have asked might KNOW the LAW ---

So be it I AM-

Sananda

Recorded by Sister Thedra of the Emerald Cross

44

I Bring with Me...

Beloved Ones -- While it is the time of communicating by this method - this means - I say unto thee - let this be recorded - that others might see and know that there is such communication -- And they shall give heed unto that which is recorded -- And for this is it given ---

When one has been called out from amongst "them" – they are not of them longer --They say that which is of the Light -- They walk upright -- They give credit unto the Father for their BEING - and unto Him credit for the LAW which I bring unto thee (the law which no man shall nullify - or set aside) ---

Now I say unto thee: - Wherein is it said that they shall not kill?

Wherein have they transgressed this law?

Wherein have they loved one another?

Wherein have they pilfered the fortune of other nations?

Wherein have they been perfect in the sight of the "Great Council"?

Wherein have they thought themself wise?

I say unto them: "Ye Bigots"! - Ye Bigots! -- Plunder no more thine brothers lands --Pilfer no more their fortune -- Give heed unto Mine Words - and let not thine foot slip ---

For it is NOW COME when the MIGHTY COUNCIL shall take ACTION! - and it shall set straight that which hast been made crooked! ---

I bring with Me A MIGHTY HOST-- I bring with the POWER and AUTHORITY --

I bring with Me MERCY and JUDGEMENT -- I KNOW the LAW and I abide thereby -- Yet the Law is JUST -- And it is given unto Me to KNOW MERCY -- So be it I shall show Mercy in ALL Mine dealings ---

Yet I say: - THEY shall cry out against Me -- And they shall curse the elements - and be as the ones which torment their brothers -- And they shall find no place wherein to lay their head -- So be it I say unto "thee" - be ye no part of them - for they shall be as ones removed into a far corner - and they shall no more torment MINE PEOPLE -- I speak unto then which have ears to hear - eyes to see - for none other shall hear or see -- I have said: "See ye the hand of GOD MOVE" -- For it shall surely MOVE - SWIFTLY and PERFECTLY - toward the end - which is perfect - and in BALANCE according unto the LAW - the PERFECT LAW - which I bring ---

I Am come that there BE LIGHT -- SEE IT - BEHOLD ITS ACTION - BE YE ONE WITH IT - AND THERE SHALL BE PEACE ---- Sananda speaks on the LAW - which IS and EVER SHALL BE ---

So be it - I AM HE –

Recorded by Sister Thedra

46

Wherein Must Thou Looked for Me?

Sori Sori -- Wherein is it written that ye shall bear witness of Me? -- Wherein is it said that ye shall follow Me? -- And is not lawful? --

I ask of thee - wherein hast thou looked for - Me - for Peace - for Light? ---

I say unto thee - thou hast wondered far afield -- looking afar for Me - for Peace - for Light -- Yet I Am not afar off - neither have I been! ---

It is said: Look neither here nor there - for I AM WITH YOU -- IT IS SO --- So be ye mindful of ME - and know ye that I AM nearer that thine hand and thine foot --- So be it that I AM the Lord of Old -- I AM the Lord of Yester-year -- I AM the Lord of TODAY -- I AM the Lord of Tomorrow --

I CHANGE NOT --

I AM THAT I AM ---

I COME that ye might KNOW ME - that ye might be prepared to go where I GO -- So let it BE ---

I AM - Sananda

Recorded by Sister Thedra of the Emerald Cross

Excerpts from - And Then the Angels Came to the First Grade Children

Foreword: I was in Los Angeles in July 1964 to attend Saint Germain's Golden Age Conference, conducted by The Summit Lighthouse of Washington, D. C. On the way to the first session friends told me that angels had visited the six-year-old children in the first grade, taught by Mrs. Baker, in a private school in Los Angeles County, California.

What? A visitation of the angels in this day? and here? A great wave of joy and happiness surged through me, in anticipation of hearing more of this story. And, as in answer to prayer, I found myself seated next to Mrs. Baker at several of The Summit Lighthouse sessions.

"Yes," she related in answer to my questions, "it was about a month before the close of the school year, just after the last big test; we had just finished our devotional exercises that morning, when all at once the children cried out: 'Teacher! Teacher! Angels! Lots and lots of Angels!'

"Of the 31 children in my class, all except three could see the angels and talk with them. The angels said they had come because we had sent so much love up to them."

Many details of this wonderful happening poured from her lips. Fairies had come with the angels. After the first day, angels and fairies continued to come every day until the close of the school year. Jesus, Mother Mary, and the Archangel Michael visited them also.

How had this great experience come about? What did the devotional service consist of? What songs were sung? What did she teach the children? Many would want to know the answers-- teachers, parents--all who are charged with the responsibility of guiding spiritually gifted children. Would she write down this story while it was still fresh in her mind?

Mrs. Baker graciously consented; and what follows is the account in her own words. As you follow the selections in the devotional service you will be aware of the joy, love and adoration expressed therein. In her words, "Our theme was, in reality, love! Love for all mankind; love for all creatures and growing things, and especially love for all the Heavenly Beings."

Helen E. MacDonald, Ph.D.

In the private religious school where I was teaching first grade in 1963-64, it was the general practice to open the day with a devotional exercise. First, we pledged allegiance to the Bible, and this was followed immediately by the pledge of allegiance to the Christian flag, and then to the American flag. Then we repeated the Lord's Prayer.

The children were taught the first and last verses of "Adoration to the Angels," p. 2, Summit Lighthouse Songbook, sung to the melody of "Away in a Manger."

Adoration to the Angels

Dear angels, bright angels now hov'ring above,

Are watching, protecting, and guiding with love,

Dear angels of heaven, our songs rise to thee,

In quiet communion thy beauty we see.

Then one day dear angels, we'll rise up to thee,

To dwell in the realms of sweet ecstasy,

We then shall ascend borne on light's shining ray

Majestic, triumphant, bring in the New Day.

Prayer

O, Our loving Heavenly Father, blessed angels, and Archangels, Blessed Jesus and Beloved Mother Mary: Please take our love and spread it over the whole world; fill the hearts of all the Communists full of love; send tons and tons of love to fill the hearts of their leaders so that they can think only of love this day. We thank you, we bless you, we adore you (this line repeated 9 times) in Jesus' name. Amen.

In teaching the children about Jesus, these thoughts were stressed: His infinite love; that He gave up His life to prove that Life is everlasting; that we are here to learn to live rightly and to glorify God, and that if we do not learn this lesson and the proof thereof here and now, we will be forced to learn it after we leave the earth; and that Jesus has prepared a place for all who follow Him each day in faith and in love expressed to all.

Our theme was, in reality, love! Love for all mankind; love for all creatures and growing things; and especially love for all the Heavenly Beings.

And Then the Angels Came!

It was just following the last big test of the year, with approximately one month of school left, that something wonderful happened in our classroom. It was on a Thursday morning (May 28, 1964). We had just finished our praise, adoration, and what had become an invocation service, when simultaneously the children cried out: "Teacher! Teacher! Angels! Angels! Lots and lots of angels!" As the children saw them, their glowing faces reflected the glory of the angels, and the wondrous scenes they beheld. With happy, vibrant voices they described what they saw.

Flowers, diamond lights, and even golden ladders were showered down on the children. "Teacher," they asked, "can we climb up these ladders into heaven?" Colors of the rainbow appeared; and a beautiful garden was placed in the front of the room on the upper wall. This garden remained there, not only during this day, but as long as the school term lasted; and often the children saw some angelic being walking in this garden. One morning they saw Jesus and Archangel Michael walking there.

The children described the angels as we have seen them pictured by the great master artists. Later, they drew pictures of them on the board. One or two children drew cherub figures--they were pink or blue, and had wings. There was much light.

The figures seemed very distinct to the children. There was a luminous radiance around them.

Every day thereafter, following their initial visitation, the angels came; and fairies (elementals) came with the angels. Both the angels and the fairies talked with the children; many times an angel or a fairy would speak individually to a child.

The children were told by both the angels and the fairies that they had come because we had sent so much love up to them. We were told to continue, even to step up the sending of Love; and we were called upon several times during the day to sing a song of love, or one of patriotism. After the first day, we always asked the angels what songs they would like to have us sing, and we always were given an answer. "The Presence of God is There" was requested several times; also "Up From the Grave He Arose." One little girl said that Jesus told her that we must sing it often (May 29th).

An Angel announced to one little girl that Mother Mary was coming. Then Mary came and spoke to her. This child then told me: "Teacher, Mary said I was the one who had wiped the tears from her eyes, on Golgotha."

One child said: "Teacher, an angel wants to talk with me and with ----- " (giving the name of another child who had some difficulty in learning). Of course, I gave my permission for these two children to go to the back of the room and talk with the angel. The angel told the child with the learning problem that he would be able to learn more rapidly from that time on. And it was so!

One fairy requested a little boy to make a swing for her; which he did at home, bringing it to school the next day. The fairies were mostly in or around the flowers, but sometimes they perched on the children, and even on the teacher!

On May 29th the children were shown the American flag with gold stripes in place of the red, symbolizing the illumination of peace which would replace war and bloodshed in the coming age.

On June 1 and 2 there were waterfalls and a beautiful rainbow in the room. Two or three days later, letters floated down to several of the children. The message to each particular child who received one, was "I Love You!"

Of the 31 six-year-old children in my room, all but three were able to see and to converse with the angels and the fairies; two of these three believed what the other children described they saw and heard. Only one child was skeptical.

The children were cautioned to "keep these things in their hearts," and not to talk about the wonderful happenings that were taking place to those who would not understand. Two of the children did tell their mothers. Fortunately, they were mothers with understanding hearts, and they, too, believed. The children used good judgment and discretion.

During one chapel period (June 4th) the speaker talked to the school children assembled there about angels. He added, "Of course, no one ever sees them." My six-year-old children looked at me, and it was all they could do to keep silent! The angels were also there!

One day (June 5th) an Angel appeared to the children and said: "The Communists want to destroy Washington; call for its protection." We sang the last verse of "My Country 'Tis of Thee" --over and over at least twenty times. I was somewhat anxious because of the apparent urgency of the message, and was leading the singing rather lustily. An Angel interrupted to speak to a child, who then said to me, "Teacher, the Angel says not to sing so loud." So we continued, more softly.

Another day (June 10th) there was a charge of golden light, which momentarily blinded the children. Two days later, there was a heavy, or rather a prolonged charge of violet light, which rendered them unable to see for quite a few minutes.

On the 17th of June, there was a general convocation of all the classes. Before going to the church building for this service, I requested the children to sing "Holy, Holy, Holy" followed by "To the Seven Archangels," verses 1 and 2. This they did, earnestly and without haste. In the church, the members of my class sat in one long row in the right wing of the edifice. During the service, all of my children (except the three) saw Archangel Michael and His Angels "cutting free" the Communists.

These are some of the most vivid of the incidents described by the children. There were many more.

M. Baker

Addendum: We sat in silence for a long time. There were tears in the eyes of Mrs. Baker as she related this story--tears of love and gratitude that this blessed experience--lasting many days--had come to her and to the beloved children in her class. Although she herself had not seen or heard the Angels, fairies and Divine Beings who came, she was aware that she had been divinely guided in teaching and leading these spiritually gifted children.

There were tears in my eyes, too, as I listened to this account of the glorious fulfillment NOW (1964) and here (in Los Angeles, City of the Angels) of the age-old promise that there would again be close communion between men and Angels in this Golden Age we are entering. Surely, it was faith in the reality of God, and in the reality of His spiritual helpers--the Angels, Archangels, Ascended Masters, and in the reality of the Elemental Kingdom--that had set the pattern to which the children had responded.

The great Archangel Michael Himself has told us that faith is contagious, as are all of the qualities of God. He has also told us how to open the door to the presence of the Angels--through love; for their world is the world of God's love and thus the only way to "entertain Angels" is to be love, to live love, and to invoke love-- love that is peace and compassion for all life; love that is without dissimulation; love which stands in the vanguard of true spiritual freedom to defend the right of every man to be all that his Maker has intended for him.

The first grade children in the class taught by Mrs. Baker, in their childlike simplicity and devotion, through their daily outpouring of consecrated love to the Heavenly Hosts, had sustained a focus of purity through which "the angels cane." With greater understanding I recalled the words of Jesus: "Unless ye become as little children, ye shall in no wise enter the kingdom of heaven," (Matthew 18:3)

55

and "Suffer the little children to come unto me, and forbid them not: for of such is the kingdom of God."

(Mark 10:14)   --H.E.M.

They Shall Obey the LAW First & Last

Beloved Ones -- This day let it be recorded that ALL might see that which I say unto thee -- There is great <u>stress</u> upon the people of ALL the lands - and they know not whither to go - that they might find Peace -- Yet it is said that they shall find NO peace - until it is established <u>within their hearts</u> ---

They have not established peace within themselves -- The transgressors are the transgressors still! - and yet these are the ones which sit in high places and <u>talk</u> of peace! ---

I say unto them - <u>they shall obey the Law first and last</u> -- Then they shall find that others shall find their way unto the council table -- First - I have given unto them the Law that they shall abide by "<u>Thou shalt NOT Kill</u>"---

They have gone their own way - heading not the law -- Yet I say the Law is exacting - it IS THE LAW - "<u>They which take up arms against their brother shall perish by their own weapons.</u>" So shall it be - for it IS THE LAW -- Let it be said that when a man speaks of peace - yet he hath no love within his heart for his fellow man - is no indication that Peace is established within him - for he fears his enemies - his part which he has fortuned unto himself -- He has not <u>known Peace</u> - for it is NOT WITHIN HIM -- Let it be said - <u>that</u> peace(?) is the part which they have given unto the poor(?) -- The poor in spirit know not peace - for they have not <u>known</u> ME -- They deny Me -- For this are they poor in spirit -- I say poor are they - they know Me not ---

Yet they shall call upon Me saying:- Lord - Lord - give us Peace! - while they but make a mockery of Mine Name -- I say they know Me not ---

So be it I say unto them - be ye accountable unto the Law - and responsible for thine own actions/ words/ deeds - then I shall hear thine petitions -- So let them which have ears to hear - hear that which I say unto them ---

I AM Sananda

the Lord thy God -

Recorded by Sister Thedra of the Emerald Cross

Soran Speaks of Sananda & Himself

Holy - Holy is the Word of God - Holy - Pure and simple is His Word -- Make ye ready thineself to receive His Word - which shall profit all which shall receive it unto themself -- For He hast given of <u>Himself</u> that they might be lifted up -- So be it that ALL which seek the Light shall receive of Him -- So let it BE -- I Am come that I might add Mine Light unto His - that there be <u>Greater</u> Light within the Earth ---

I say unto thee: There are ones within thine midst which hast come for that purpose - and it is Mine part to give unto thee this Word ---

57

There are ones which have no knowledge of Me - neither the Lord God - OR THE FATHER Which hast sent Us -- While they know not - it differs not with Us -- We come seeking not recognition of men -- We come solely because of Our Love and Compassion for them - that they might be brought out of bondage - that they might have freedom as We know freedom -- So be it I Am One of the Eloheim - and I give of Mine Light - Mine Love that they might come into the place wherein ALL things are known -- So be it that I Am He which hast waited long for this part - for this time when the Sons of God shall gather themselves together as One Nation - as One People - as One Church - as One Mighty Council -- And I say unto thee - this is the action for which we work -- This is the Action taken that there be Peace within the world of men - amongst all men -- Yet the ones which are not responsible for themself shall be removed - and they shall be replaced - with the ones which have become responsible ---

I say unto them -- Be ye as ones responsible for all thine actions - all thine deeds - all thine fortune which thou hast fortuned unto thine own self -- So be it the Law ---

I speak this day that they might know that which I say unto them -- So be it that the way is now clear before thee - that ye might come into the place wherein there is no darkness - no mystery - no fear - no danger - no want - no death - no hatred - only Light -- And therein is Love - Pure and Holy in Its Purity -- They shall rejoice and be made glad -- So be it and Selah ---

I AM Soran

Recorded by Sister Thedra of the Emerald Cross

58

The Lord God of Old

Beloved ones -- While it is yet time - let it be understood that there are many which cry: Lord! Lord! Yet they know Me not!

I say unto thee: I AM the Lord of Old! -- I AM THE LORD COD OF OLD! -- I AM the Lord God of Yesterday - Today - and Tomorrow -- I AM HE - Which is SENT OF MINE FATHER that He might be GLORIFIED IN ME - THROUGH HE - and BY ME - that the Earth and the Children thereof be lifted up -- So be it that I AM the same - Yesterday - Today - and FOREVER -- I AM no less for bringing Mineself unto thee -- I AM no more for going unto Mine Father -- For I AM HE -- The Father and I are ONE -- And it is said: "Man Know Thineself and ye shall know ME - The Lord thy God" -- So shall it be -- For this do I REVEAL MINESELF at this time -- I say: Awaken ALL ye Children of the Earth! -- Awaken ALL YE NATIONS of the Earth! For it is now come when ye shall be brought to account for thineself ---

I speak unto thee that it be so -- So let it BE ---

I AM

Sananda

Recorded by Sister Thedra of the Emerald Cross

The Bigots & Fools - They Think to Deceive Me?

Sananda Speaking -- It shall be for the benefit of them which seek the Light - that I speak unto thee -- Let that which I say unto thee be recorded thusly: ---

There are ones which seek the Light which I AM -- There are ones which run after strange gods - and these are the ones which believe Me not -- I say they seek afar - they know not that I AM COME! ---

I say these are the unknowing ones ---

While they know Me not - I say unto thee - thou knowest Me - and it is fortuned unto thee to follow after Me -- So be it that I bid them "Follow ye Me" - Yet they hear not! -- They ask of men - and they put words into Mine mouth - Which I spit out! - for I do not put Mine foot into a hole -- I KNOW The pitfalls -- I say unto thee - hear ye that which I say - and thou hearest Me - yet they are deaf - they are as ones prone to bigotry and selfishness - and they think themself wise -- They fret for small things -- They fear the Light - knowing only the darkness -- They hide themself - that they might not be known unto Me -- They think to deceive ME???

I say they KNOW ME NOT! -- While I Am come that they might know - they are prone to the learning of books -- They pilfer their sayings - and speak as the machine and know not the meaning of the words they prattle so freely - that they might be justified in their dealing - in their frailties -- I say they are wont to justify their injustice - their bigotry - their frailties and foolishness -- Poor foolish mortals they be ---

I say these shall come to know their frailties - and they shall find no justification in Mine sight -- They shall not be justified by LAW - for there is no law which justifies these things - them which betray themself -- So be it that I have spoken freely and fearlessly about - and unto the BIGOTS - the FOOLS -- For it shall be given unto Me to set them straight -- So be it I AM COME that they might have Light -- So be it - it is the way of the Initiate to give of Himself that others be delivered out of bondage ---

So let it BE as the Father hast willed it --

I AM HE Which is sent that there BE LIGHT ---

I AM Sananda

Recorded by Sister Thedra of the Emerald Cross

The Age of Awakening... It Shall NOT be Painless

Has it not been written that this day shall bring forth <u>great</u> <u>stress/</u> great weariness/ great learning/ great knowledge - and a "wayward generation" - out of which shall come the greatest leaders known unto men -- It shall be the "<u>Age of Awakening</u>" - and the awakening shall <u>not</u> be painless!

Yet it is given unto Me to see them wandering hither and yon seeking of men - asking for opinions - seeking verifications of their own opinions ---

Now these shall find that they are misled - mis-guided -- They have betrayed themself - for they have not sought TRUTH from the FOUNTAIN HEAD -- They have added unto the darkness of ages past - their own -- And they have become so burdened down with their dogmas and creeds that they can no longer find the "Kernels of Wheat" which is hidden within the ASH -- I say the "ash" for it is now come when they shall search the <u>ash</u> for that which is left! ---

61

Now ye shall give this unto them that they might come to know - they shall <u>first</u> seek TRUTH from THE SOURCE - and then they shall KNOW for a surety -- They shall be given as they are capable of receiving -- So be it that I KNOW their capacity ---

While it is given unto Me to be the Lord God - sent of Mine Father that they be lifted up - I see them as ones willful and wanting -- They deny Me - Mine Word - Mine Servants - Mine Messengers - Mine Emissaries ---

I tell the of a surety that these shall come to know that they have betrayed themself -- They shall fall by the way bruised - sick of heart - fearful and disillusioned - And then they shall cry out - Lord! Lord! - and they shall come to know that they have been given a "bare bone" - that they have found thereon no nourishment - nothing to sustain them in the time of stress - nothing to give unto them freedom from bondage -- And as a last resort they shall cry out for their "Idol" - they shall bury their face in their hands - and cry aloud for surcease from their grief - for they shall have such as they cannot bear alone -- I say they shall cry out even as the cry of the frightened child -- They shall prostrate themself before their empty shrines and cry aloud - Lord! Lord! hear ye our petitions - and give unto us comfort for we are spent!!

Then they shall REMEMBER that which I have said unto them ---

I say unto them: TURN UNTO THE LIGHT - SEEK YE THE LIGHT WHICH I AM - and give unto Me credit for Being that which I AM ---

When they come unto Me with a contrite heart - filled with LOVE - And when they are wont to turn from their ways of darkness - I shall receive them unto Mine-Self and make of them servants - and they shall first accept Me as their own Lord God - and THEN - I shall touch them - and they shall KNOW ME as the SON of the ALMIGHTY FATHER Which hast sent ME ---

I AM that I AM -

Sananda

I Am The Door!

Beloved Ones -- This day let it be said that the ones which do revile against Me - shall come to see that there is no other way in which they enter into the Holy of Holies -- I say I AM the WAY/ I AM the door through which they enter -- None enter save through ME - for I AM the DOOR---

I AM HE Which is Guardian of the Portal - and none enter unknown unto Me ---

I AM HE Which KNOWS the thoughts of men -- I see their deeds which they are wont to hide from Me -- The poor of spirit - these are impoverished - and they know Me not ---

Let it be recorded that I AM COME that they might come into the place wherein I abide -- Yet these poor of spirit "Know not that I AM COME" - They ask of men? They question of men? - they search of the learned -- They seek the answers within the pages of history -- Yet they find no satisfaction -- They are not as yet awakened -- I say they have <u>as</u> <u>yet</u> not awakened - for they are as yet asleep! ---

Let it be said that they too shall awaken in due season - and they shall be glad their sleep is past -- Let it be said that they shall ripen as the fruit on the Vine - then I shall pluck them out - and they shall serve Me - and they shall be glad -- So be it that I have spoken - and thou hast heard Me ---

I AM Sananda

Recorded by Sister Thedra of the Emerald Cross

The Responsibility of Ones in High Places

--Soran

Soran Speaking -

Beloved ones -- This day let us consider the great responsibility of the ones which sit in "high" places -- These are responsible for the conduct of themself - as well as the ones over which they preside ---

Now it is given unto thine people to call themself free - "A FREE PEOPLE" -- Wherein have they been free? ---

Wherein have they free speech?

-freedom of action?

I say they know <u>not</u> freedom! -- They but <u>think</u> themself free -- While they are bound by flesh/ by the law of gravity (?) - by the

64

attraction of the Moon - by the tides - by mans opinion - his actions - and for the most part their own legirons! ---

Yea - I say unto them - they know not freedom -- Yet - they shall endure greater bondage 'ere they know the freedom of which I speak ---

They have accumulated many legirons - many - many laws have they made for themself - which they shall be responsible for -- They have not obeyed the Law which wast given unto them from the beginning -- They have transgressed the first Law -- This is the pity - While they revile against the ones which transgress the law which they are wont to make and enforce - they have transgressed ALL the "Commandments" given unto them! ---

I say unto them: "Be ye responsible for that which ye set into motion - and be ye without blemish" -- Be ye spotless of character - - Let thine Light so shine that ALL might honor thee - and know that thou art of good character -- Be ye not tainted with/ or by the wonton of fornication - the fornication which is giver unto them in high places of thine society ---

Be ye clean or hands - and be ye pure of thought -- Let not thine hand be swift to pull down the "Standard of the Crown and the Cross" - shall it not be thine deliverance? -- Be ye swift to uphold law and justice - the LAW of which I speak ---

For it is the LAW OF JUSTICE - and no man is to be excluded - or exempt - for their position or Earthly stature ---

I say - because of position in "high places" they shall not be exempt -- These shall be the beacon lights -- These shall be the pillars of Government -- These shall walk as ones <u>sober</u> - as ones justified -- And they shall be beyond reproach -- For I say - they shall serve well their fellow man - their Brethren - impartially and without malice or prejudice ---

I say these shall be given a part within the Government of the Earth - and therein shall be placed the ones which shall set straight that which hast been made crooked -- So be it the hypocrites shall be removed into a corner - and they shall learn well their lesson -- For this shall they be given a <u>lesser</u> part -- It is said "Pity is the one which betrays himself/ or his trust." So it is ---

I come that ye might know that which is designed - that which shall come to pass -- Yet each and every one shall be responsible for his part within the "NEW ORDER" -- I say none shall shirk his responsibility -- So be it that I have spoken unto <u>thee</u> -- Pass not the "Word" until thou hast considered well thine own responsibility!

I AM Soran

(This is given at a time when the actions or high ranking politicians are being questioned)

Deliverance of The Earth

-Sananda

Beloved Ones -- This day I say unto thee - it is <u>now</u> come when there shall be great stress upon the "Peoples" of the EARTH - yea - and the Earth -- For She shall seethe and tear from Her stress -- She shall tilt and roll -- She shall be as a ship tossed about at sea - for She goes thru turbulent waters - <u>and She knows no fear</u> - yet She groans under

66

Her burden - For She too is ensculed in matter -- Matter is HER CROSS ---

She is given unto patience - yet She cries out for deliverance ---

Now when it is come that She goes forth into Her new orbit - She shall be free from the suffering and torment which is fortuned unto Her now -- Wherein is it said - "She shall have a new berth?" ((Prophesies of Other Worlds - and The Scripts)) -- Now it shall be fortuned unto Her to throw off Her yoke - and the laggards shall no longer ride Her back -- I say unto thee - She shall be free of the LAGGARDS - and no more shall She give unto them footing -- So be it I Am come that She too might be assisted in Her INITIATION - in Her "RAISING" -- So let it be - for I Am the Lord God sent of Mine Father that it be done according unto the Law -- So be it and Selah ---

I AM Sananda

Recorded by Sister Thedra of the Emerald Cross

...A New Generation – They Shall Go to War No More -

Beloved Ones -- This day let it be understood that service unto ones country is not enough - it is not sufficient unto thine salvation ---

For to love one another is without counterpart -- It is the greatest of all "Service" -- Service unto thine brother-men - men of thine own - which are like unto thee - these are thine own kind -- Yet there is MORE -- Consider well; who is thine Brother? - Wherein is the other excluded for reason that he has his habitat in a foreign land? -

67

or that he wears a garment of another color? -- I say unto thee - "LOVE ye one another - and thou shall NOT KILL!"---

While it is now come that they shall raise up against an unjust system - and great persecution - I say unto the oppressed - and the down trodden - "A new Generation shall be raised up - which shall go to war no more - they shall bring about a NEW ORDER - a NEW SYSTEM - and war shall be outlawed -- So be it according unto the Will of Mine Father which hast sent Me ---

I speak out this day as One sent that there be Light in the world of men -- I say a NEW GENERATION shall be raised up - and they shall NO MORE GO TO WAR! -- So be it I have spoken - and I shall speak again and again -- I shall raise Mine Voice against the oppressors and the ones which sit in high places - and think themself WISE! ---

So be it I AM the Lord thy God

San Anda -

Recorded by Sister Thedra or the Emerald Cross

Swift Action - The Mighty Council

Beloved: - It is Mine part to give unto thee this Word - and it shall be thine part to give it unto "Them" -- For it is now come when they shall be torrented by the opposing forces - and there are many -- I say unto thee the opposing force hast no mercy - no ethic - and it is not in any way of that nature -- I tell thee of a surety that the opposing forces - which do exist - are of the nether world - and it is not or the Light ---

There are ones which have given of themself completely and devotedly that they might destroy that which hast been done within the realms of Light -- I tell thee the time is come when ye shall see the forces of darkness put down -- For "We of the Mighty Council" are not of a mind to stand by and see the Work of Our hand devoured by the force which they send forth! ---

We shall move swiftly! - and silently -- We shall give no quarter unto them - for We ask none of them - that is - nothing save obedience unto the Law!

This is the time for ACTION! - and ACT We shall!

It is Mine part to give unto them the Law - the forewarning - and to carry out the GREAT AND DIVINE PLAN --

Now I say unto thee: "Stand ye steadfast - knowing wherein thou art staid - for I Am come that ye know - that ye might be sustained -- So let it be - for the good of all that I have COME unto thee ---

Be ye blest as I have been blest --

I AM the Lord thy God -

Sananda

Recorded by Sister Thedra of the Emerald Cross

The Powers of Darkness Shall Not Put Down 'Mine Banner'

Holy - Holy is the Word - and great the power thereof -- I say unto thee GREAT is the POWER thereof -- And Mine Word shall be

69

heard - and It shall bear GREAT FRUIT - and they shall <u>know</u> that it hast gone forth as a POWER in the LANDS of the EARTH ---

The powers of darkness shall not put down "Mine Banner" - for I shall raise up a people which shall carry it high - and uphold its standard -- I tell thee of a surety that I Am not to be put into a corner -- Neither am I to be silent -- For I see the need of Light in the dark places -- I see the darkness go forth as a power - which would consume them - were it not possible for Us of the Mighty Council to take action ---

It is by DIVINE COMMAND that we do so - and it shall be for the GOOD of ALL ---

There shall be a great <u>clash</u> of <u>Powers</u> - and the elements shall do their part -- And the waters shall be divided - and the ones which serve ME shall walk upon dry land - dry shod -- And they shall know no fear - for they shall know wherein they are staid -- So be it I speak unto thee now in symbolic form - that ye might understand that which I say unto thee -- The two powers shall be divided in two parts - the Light - the dark - and they shall clash - and great shall be the action -- Yet ye shall stand steadfast - knowing that thou art of the Light -- And I say unto thee - thine feet shall not be caught in the mire -- So be it that I <u>know</u> that which I say unto thee ---

So let it suffice that I AM

The Lord thy God

Sananda

Recorded by Sister Thedra of the Emerald Cross

...And No Man Shall Lose his Life - Rather Shall He Find It

Sori Sori -- This day I would say unto thee - Behold the Work which I shall do -- The work which I shall do shall differ from that of the WAR-mongers - for I shall set up Mine Banner on their battle fields - and I shall call from out their ranks men which shall give unto Me credit for Being That Which I AM ---

I shall appoint then MINE GUARDIANS of TRUTH and JUSTICE - and they shall turn from the wars which men hast fortuned unto themself - and these shall follow ME - and keep the Law Which I bring -- They shall be as Mine Servants - for they shall serve Me with their whole heart -- And they shall likewise serve their fellow ren - with LOVE and JUSTICE for ALL ---

I SAY:

I shall recruit from the ranks of men - ones which shall be lifted up -- And these shall never again give unto their Brother the bitter cup -- For they shall know that they but drink from the same cup -- So be it I have spoken out against the "War-mongers and oppressors" -- Now I say - I shall set straight the WAY before them - and they which hear Mine Voice shall obey Mine commandment - COME! COME ye out from amongst them and glorify the Father Which hast sent ME ---

So be it that Mine Army shall march forth unto a GREAT VICTORY -- So be it I shall lead them ---

And no man shall lose his life -- Rather shall he find it ---

I AM The Lord thy God

Sananda

Recorded by Sister Thedra of the Emerald Cross

Now I Come Declaring

Sori Sori -- by Mine Grace shall ye be given that which shall profit thee -- ye shall first seek the LIGHT and ye shall not be deceived. Ye shall be as one responsible for the Word which is given unto thee thru this Mine handmaiden, for she hast proven herself trustworth - - and I find her trustworth in all things.

Be ye aware of Mine Word which is given unto thee thru and by this manner for it is good and I have declared it so -- so be it. Let thine tongue be swift to bear witness of Me, Mine Word and Mine servant for I have claimed the Word, the Work perfect, so be it and Selah. I say ye shall find no fault with the method in which it is given, for it is given in such a manner that it shall profit thee to accept it.

I say: HOLY IS THE WORD -- and I declare it so!

Be ye blest to receive it, for this I give it unto thee.

Now I come declaring unto thee this day, that I have raised up one which I have given the power and the authority to speak for me -- I have given her Mine name that ye might have the knowledge which hast been kept for this day -- while I say there shall come ones declaring that they are mine anointed ones with the authority to speak Mine words -- I say that I know who is who -- and what is what! I say many are called and few are chosen -- this one I have called -- this one I have chosen. I have chosen her for her capacity

72

to learn of Me -- I have chosen her for her desire to follow Me. I have chosen her for her willingness to follow Me -- there is not any deceit within her -- there is no envy or malice within her -- yet, I say into her: "COME UP HIGHER FOR I HAVE GREATER THINGS IN STORE FOR THEE". She goes where sent and comes when called.

I have placed upon her head Mine hand and I have blest her, and she hast responded unto Mine touch -- she hast rested not on her laurels. She hast wasted not her talent which I have given unto her at the altar of the Lord thy God.

I say unto thee: hear ye Me and ye shall NOT put words into Mine mouth -- neither shall ye pilfer Mine words. Ye shall not deny Mine servant -- for to deny her is to deny Me. So be it I see them cry out against Mine servant while they claim to be following Me! I say unto them: "THOU HAST NOT SEEN ME, NEITHER HEARD ME". I am come that they might know the true from the false, so let them see the LIGHT which I AM, and I say unto thee: I shall shew Mineself unto them which do seek the Light and come unto Me as a little child, clean of hand and heart.

Put thine hand in mine and I shall lead thee. Come and we shall walk together and rejoice for our communication, so be it as the Father would have it. Amen and Amen.

Recorded by Sister Thedra

March 8, 1974

Mt. Shasta, California

The following explanations and definitions of terms used by Sananda (Jesus) and the various Sibors were given by Sananda through direct revelation, July 17, 1964. They are not alphabetical. These explanations should be read over and over.

"My Beloved Sibors please give us plainly the definitions of the following words that there may be no error on our part." – Thedra.

THEMSELF? - What is the explanation of your terminology of "Themself" - themselves? –

"I (Sananda) say unto thee mine beloved, they which would be unto thee a vessel, unto thee a sibor, unto thee teacher, are as ones enlightened of the Father, enlightened of the Father for the light is in them. They know their parts well, they have their memory, they have mastered the elements, they can do all the things which I do and they take unto "themself" no credit for they have overcome self. They are self-less. Now I say unto them: them which work with thee are the Selfless ones. They ask no thing for "themself." Now while this is true they are as one.

They are within the great brotherhood of the Selfless Ones - the Ones clothed in white. They are as the Royal Assembly - and each unto his own, yet each for all and all for one. Now while in thy world, they (of thy world) are selfish and they are not for the whole - they ask for self and I speak of these as the selfish ones. I speak unto them in terms which they shall come to know and therein is wisdom. I say that they shall be responsible for "themself" and as a world of men I say they shall be responsible for their society; they "themself" have created it. Now I speak unto thee mine beloved, I say ye shall be responsible for thyself. He shall be responsible for himself. They as a whole shall be responsible for that which they have created, while thou art responsible unto thyself for thine part - and not held accountable for theirs. Be it so."

BELEIS? "Mighty is the word and great the power thereof. I say unto thee this word carries with it the part of surrender. The word is the release of power - that which is sent forth by the one which asks of the Father His blessing. It is the surrender of the self - the complete surrender of the personal will and letting the Father's will be accomplished is all things through thee. "So be it" - it the accomplishment, the acceptance of the Father's plan."

SELAH? - "The word carries the Seal of Truth - meaning it is without error - no mistake - it is the verification of Truth - not subject to change."

SIBET? - "The Sibet is one which has offered or presented himself as a candidate for the greater learning and for the greater initiation and he comes as an empty vessel that he may be filled. So be it."

SIBOR? - "I am the Sibor of Sibors." - "The Sibor is one which has been illumined of God the Father. He has returned unto the Father purified. He has gone the Royal Road - which means he has overcome death. He has mastered the lower elements - he controls the elements. He can raise the dead - heal the sick - he can create like unto the Father for he has finished his course and won the victory and returned unto the Father the Victor. So be it."

"I am the Sibor of Sibors. I am the first born of Him which hast sent me. Sananda."

LEGIRONS? - "Beloved - I say unto thee: thy opinions and thy dogmas are not the least of these - neither thy creeds. Be it ever that these are great and heavy ones. Now let it be understood that a leg-iron is something which holds thee bound. It is something which holds thee, it keeps thee fast, wherein progress is not possible. Now that progress be made possible, ye shall cut away the legirons. Knowest thou these bound by legirons? These are to be pitied, they drag them with them impeding their progress - and they are as ones bound! They are not free - are they? While they serve their sentence - they are as ones bound - they are bond-men - they are bound men - men bound. Now let me say I too am a "bondsman." I come that they may be free. I say I bring unto thee the law which thou shall obey - unto the letter - then I shall give unto thee that which I have kept for thee. Be ye as one prepared for that."

PREPARATION? Now - preparation - what do you mean by "preparation?" "This my beloved is the part which they shall do - the part of preparation is: cleaning thyself of all the opinions, indoctrinations of man. The cup must be emptied. This is thy part, the becoming the "little child" unopinionated, unscathed and unmarred with or by their doctrines, creeds, and crafts. I say the child is undoctrinated and unopinionated and is the virgin mind - (yet it does not remain so, long in this world). While the little child represents the empty cup - the empty vessel, the Virgin Spirit, it is given unto the child to be one which has come from other realms and to have been in many embodiments, many times: yet the symbol of virginity. Wherein is it said there are none innocent among thee?

76

WHEREIN I AM? - "Now while thou art yet within the world of men - I am within mine Father's realm, the place wherein there is no darkness, wherein ALL things are known. I say wherein ALL things are known, wherein there is No mystery. And too - I say when thou hast attained unto thy Royal Road, when thou hast become part of the Royal Assembly thou shall know as I - thou shall be as I - thou shall be brought into the place wherein I am, for I say unto thee this is attainment. This is the day of Attainment, the day of "becoming," the day of thy salvation. Know ye that this is Mine day - the day for which thou hast waited? I say unto thee this is the day of fulfillment. This is Mine Day. Mine Day is come ---"

What is meant by "ALL THE LANDS OF THE EARTH ?" - "This I mean, all the lands of the Earth. I have said it, I mean it as I have said it and there is no mystery of or to it."

ALL MANKIND? "This is Mine people - Mine children - Mine Flock - Mine Church - Mine brethren - Mine congregation unto whom I shall minister. By Mine own hand shall they be fed and led. These have I come to find.

Are not all hu-man beings considered "Man Kind"? by thine own standards. Yet all men are not of me."

WHAT DO YOU MEAN - "WILL IT SO"? - "There is power in the "WILL" and the power which they use to create their own torment and confusion is misused energy. Yet they will this - they will it so.

Now when ye will to serve me ye give unto me thy undivided attention, the whole heart - thy heart - thine ALL. Yet I say that they

77

which doth attempt to serve me with one hand, and the dragon with the other - - has not willed to serve me. They are not of me - they are not of Mine flock. I say they are either with me or against me. I cannot accept the one hand while they reserve the other for the dragon. They are not wholeheartedly mine. I make no compromises with the dragon. Mine shall come out from them and surrender unto me themself - their all - without reservation. This is willing it so - for they will the Father's will be done in them, through them, by them. They leave no energy that the dragon may use. They use all their energy to serve me. This is mine word unto thee."

WHAT IS DARKNESS? - "Thine Un-knowing - thy darkness comes from the fall of man - which one was with God the Father perfect which didst have his memory blanked from him when he didst transgress."

MAYAS VEIL? - "The result of such unknowing - the darkness which man has brought upon himself. The part he has created for himself."

WHAT DOES IT MEAN TO BETRAY ONES SELF? - "This is the sad part for first the 'fall' came from his betrayal - and it hast resulted in the fall - in the veil of Maya - the "illusion" and in thy un-knowing - in thy own darkness."

WHAT OF BETRAYING "HIS OWN TRUST"? - "The plan is all inclusive and includes all - yet there are ones unaware of the "plan" - (and they are not as included in this temple as yet) - no personal reference unto the ones within this temple.

Now when one becomes aware of his part, he is given the law and it is provided for his own good - and he has the law clearly stated, plainly recorded, and he turns his face away - that he may hide from it. He puts his fingers into his ears that he may not hear it. He gives unto his benefactors the bitter cup and he goes his own willful way. He has betrayed himself for he shall be caught up short of his course. When he has been given a chance - a "part" within the plan and he has committed himself, he has the responsibility given unto him for that "part" and should he be so foolish as to betray his trust he shall be like unto one which has thrown overboard his <u>own</u> life belt - poor foolish ones!"

WISDOM? - What is meant by the word "Wisdom?" - "Wisdom is that which is light, the knowledge of the law and its proper use. The right use of the law - and this Mine children is Mine part. I come that ye may BECOME wise! Wisdom is thy divine gift - not of man, for man of Earth is foolish indeed - and he is nothing save that which the Father has endowed him. All else is of the world of "illusion" which shall pass into nothingness in the Light which I Am."

WHAT IS THE "PEARL OF GREAT PRICE, THE PRICELESS PEARL." - "That which I offer thee - thy freedom, thy salvation from bondage - thine inheritance in full - Mine word which is not purchased with coin - not bought, neither is it sold. It is the wisdom of which I speak. Mine offer unto thee is without price - it is the 'pearl' - "Mine Pearl."

WHY ARE MIS-SPELLED AND GRAMMATICAL ERRORS USED IN THESE SCRIPTS? - "I am not a conformist. I am not concerned with the letters of man for I am He which has come that they be unbound by their fetters, I say unto them which desireth the letter - unto then the letter. I say unto thee: be ye as ones free from such bondage. I stand ready to free thee from thy bondage. Unto thee I say - give unto the letter no thought. Hear what I say for I shall say it in many ways as becomes me and serves mine purpose, I say I am no stranger in thine midst.

While they know me not, I know them. I see them bowing down before the Golden Calf - and they worship at the shrines which they have set up. (Their own standards of education.) They guild them and bring unto them burnt offerings - yet they close me out. Be ye not so foolish. Be ye not so foolish! I am come that ye might have Light - Wisdom - Freedom which is the Father's will. While the letter changeth and passeth away - and the letter is not the law - the letter is of no consequence other than to cause thee to see the "Word." The Word is the power which shall provoke thine mind into action and thy mind shall be free from the letter. See what is meant within the Word, and let thine mind be staid on me - the Light, the Way - Truth and Wisdom."

"I am He which hast come - that ye be free: forever free. I am Sananda - Son of God. Once known as the Nazarine, He which was born of Mary, Ward of Joseph.

Recorded by Thedra.

The Great Uprising

Beloved Ones -- This day let it be recorded that which shall be given unto them -- There shall be a GREAT UPRISING within the land - and it shall be the fortune of many to be as ones deprived of their vehicles - and they shall be tormented -- I say their torment shall be

fortuned unto them thru - and by the oppressors and the oppressed -
- For the two shall come together on one common ground - and they
shall stand face to face in conflict -- And it shall be the beginning of
a GREAT STRUGGLE for SUPREMACY -- I say the oppressed
shall raise up and they shall be of great strength - for they shall be
as ones which have overthrown the law - and taken unto themself
the authority -- They shall take the law into their own hands - and
there shall be GREAT and TERRIBLE VIOLENCE -- While I say
unto thee it is the beginning of a great conflict - it shall be the
beginning - and the END - for I say unto thee - "Justice shall reign
supreme" And for this do ye wait ---

Wherein has Justice been Supreme?

Wherein has Justice reigned?

And for this do I say unto thee - be ye at Peace and Poise -- Let
not thine tongue betray thee -- Be ye silent as the Sphinx - and wise
as the Serpent -- Let it suffice thee that I AM COME that there be
LIGHT - So be it - there IS LIGHT -- Be ye One with IT ---

Let no word of hatred or malice escape thine lips -- And LOVE
YE ONE ANOTHER --

Be ye blest --

For this do I come --

I AM Sananda

Recorded by Sister Thedra of the Emerald Cross

81

Sananda's Word to the Traitors

Sori Sori -- Hast not it been recorded that there shall be opposition? - And it shall come within the time which is now come -- And it shall be given unto thee to <u>know</u> the opposing forces - for they shall be as ones which have come and gone -- And the ones which have given unto thee their word of loyalty and fidelity unto the "WORD" -- I say ye shall cut them off -- And ye shall be no part of their discord - or their dishonor -- They shall be as ones CUT OFF! And they shall be as the ones which shall be of the - (the cast off traitor) - they shall have no part of thine reward - neither thine energy or blessing ---

I say I bless not the unjust!

I give not Mine blessing unto the unjust - the wayward!

I come that ALL be blest -- Yet when they do defile Mine Word - turn their face from Me - and run after <u>strange gods</u> -- I turn Mine face from them -- and I simply let them be -- So be it that I the Lord thy God does not condone the actions of the <u>hypocrites</u> and TRAITORS! -- I am not of a mind to assist them -- Yet it is said they shall CRY for Mine <u>assistance</u> -- So be it I have raised Mine Voice against them - and they shall KNOW that I have spoken ---

So be it - I AM Sananda

Recorded by Sister Thedra of the Emerald Cross

82

They will Call Themselves Innocent

Beloved Ones -- Wherein is it said that there shall be great stress upon the people -- I say unto thee great stress shall be upon them - and they shall know much suffering -- Great shall be their loss - and great shall be the weeping -- Women shall know no rest - and men shall carry their own unto their burial pyres with heavy hearts -- And they shall give unto themself no credit for their part in their suffering -- They shall call themself innocent ---

Yet I ask thee - "Wherein have they cleansed their hands -- Wherein have they been as ones without hatred - without blame?" -- Now it is come when they shall cry for surcease from their suffering - and they shall lament their lot -- So be it that they have been warned -- They have the law clearly stated -- Many have gone before them that the way be made clear before them -- Yet hatred and greed is their lot -- The pit of it -- The hatred which they have - the greed -- The pity!! ---

Such is the way of the unknowing ones -- They cry out for mercy - knowing not to whom they cry! Yet when I speak unto them they hear not - for they have not given unto Me credit for being that which I AM -- They think to tie Mine hands -- Yet I am not bound by their thinking - their opinions - their own law -- I am bound only by Mine own Word -- I say - I am BOUND by Mine WORD unto thee! I have said - "Follow ye Me and I shall lead thee out of bondage" It is for Mine LOVE solely that I come unto thee - that they might KNOW that which I say unto thee -- Give it unto them - and they shall do with it as they will -- So be it it shall profit them to turn from their hatred and sit down as BROTHERS and drink from the same chalice - bind up their wounds and count the spoils -- Let it be said they have much to learn from their loss -- Let it profit them -- For this have I spoken ---

I AM come that there be LIGHT -- So let it be

I AM Sananda - the Lord God -

Recorded by Sister Thedra of the Emerald Cross

As a Mighty Thrust

Beloved Ones -- This day let it be written - that when one asks of the Father Light - it shall not be denied him - Yet when he seeks of men he shall become confused -- For men are within the realm of men - within bondage - and they are too - working in darkness - knowing not ---

While I say unto thee - there is a Host which stands by to assist - when the Word goes forth - "Let there BE LIGHT!" -- I say it goes forth as a MIGHTY THRUST -- And it cannot be intercepted by the force of darkness -- I say it cannot be intercepted by the forces of darkness!! For it is DIRECT within its course - and strait to its point of direction ---

Let it be understood that the way has been made strait - and not one shall be unto the other a fortune - for each is a single "unit" a separate Entity/Being/Individual - and hast free will -- And at no time shall one depend upon another for his passport/into the Inner Temple -- I have said - that each one is responsible for his own passport into the Inner Temple -- While many have been sent to show the way - it is their part to point the way - and the part of each one to heed that which is LAW -- And let it be said that the dogmas

84

and creeds are mans -- not LAW - for they have bound themself by their "Creeds and Dogmas"

Let it be said that - when one sets up an Altar in his name - and makes certain laws to suit himself - designed to bind them which follow him - he has indeed portioned out for himself a "bitter cup" - - Now it is said that - "Great is the Power of the Word and Great the Manifestation thereof" -- So be it -- I give unto thee the "WORD" and it shall suffice thee -- Yet ye shall apply the Law and demand of them adherence unto it -- Let them not defile the Altar which I have set up -- Let them not contaminate the "WORD" Let them not bring forth Adulteration - which shall be unto them their sorrow -- I say unto them -- their SORROW! For to do so is pitiful! - I say to adulterate or contaminate "THE WORD" is a pitiful thing indeed! - --

So let it suffice that I have given it unto thee in this manner and it hast been recorded as given - and not one word shall be changed - - For this is it given thusly - that it STAND as Mine testimony unto them which shall follow AFTER ME -- So be it and Selah ---

I AM Sananda

Recorded by Sister Thedra of the Emerald Cross

Words of Comfort – and Promises Unfulfilled

Beloved Ones -- Wherein is it said that there shall be great suffering -- Is it not so - and when have they known Peace? -- I say unto thee they shall have Peace! -- Yet they shall first have peace within their own heart -- I say each shall establish Peace within his own heart -

85

and he shall be as one at "Peace" -- He shall look unto NO MAN to give it unto him - for it is not within any mans power to establish peace within the heart of another -- The word of "Comfort" - Promises unfulfilled - are but poor poultices --- Let Peace be established within the heart - and no man can take it from thee - for it is thine! - And it is now come when all their "Promises" and their "Pacts" shall be broken - and they shall see the foolishness of such as they are wont to look for - within the "World of Men" -- I say they shall turn unto the Light and therein they shall bind Peace -- And they shall find that they are responsible for that which hast tormented them -- I say: Let Peace be stablished within them - and NO MAN can take it from them! ---

So be it they shall seek the Light and it shall not be denied them -- So be it I have spoken unto them which doth seek Peace in the "World of Men" -- Wherein have they found Peace therein? ---

Mighty is the Word of the Lord - and GREAT the POWER thereof! - And I say unto thee -- LET PEACE be established within thee -- Let thine OWN LIGHT so shine that ALL might SEE IT and be drawn unto it ---

I AM Sananda

Recorded by Sister Thedra of the Emerald Cross

How to Find Peace

Beloved Ones -- While it is the time for rejoicing - I say unto thee -- There is great sorrow within the land -- The people are sorely oppressed - and they find no rest ---

I say they know no peace -- Yet it is given unto Me to KNOW that which torments them -- Too I know wherein their Peace lieth -- I say - they are tormented and know not that which torments them - - Let them turn from their own waywardness - their own wanton - selfishness - hatred - and they shall find peace ---

I say -- Peace shall be found within themself - for they shall first establish Peace within them - and then they shall bless themself as they would have Me bless them -- So be it I am come that they might know wherein their Peace lies -- Bless thine own self - by establishing Peace within thine self - and no man shall deny thee that gift - for it is thine by Divine right -- So accept it in the Name of the father Which hast sent Me ---

So be it - I AM

Sananda

Recorded by Sister Thedra of the Emerald Cross

Then We Shall Take Note of Them

Blest art thou O Mine Children -- Blest art thou -- Let it be - for this do I come -- I speak unto thee from out the Inner Temple wherein I abide -- I come as One sent - that I might add Mine blessing ---

For this have I waited -- This day I would say unto thee - there is a Mighty Host which has drain nigh unto the Earth - that She be lifted up -- So be it that I Am ONE of the Host - and it is given unto Me to see them which walk amongst thee - and to know their going and coming -- And it is the time for which We have waited - when they might have concourse with the Earth - and the people thereof -

87

- It is said that there has been such concourse - and it is no more -- I ask - wherein have they been schooled? Wherein have they learned such wisdom as they are so wont to expound? ---

I say that there is the concourse between thee and this place wherein We the Host abides - at no time shall the ones which <u>think</u> themself wise - pilfer the Secrets of the Inner Temple -- I say they shall prove themself and <u>then</u> We shall take note of them -- So be it I am come that they be informed - and that they might come to know that they are not alone -- I say they are <u>not</u> <u>alone</u> - for "We" have Emissaries amongst them which they know not ---

These have not the mind to betray themself -- They walk softly and gently - amongst the ones which have the mind to usurp the power and authority which is theirs -- I say - they shall not put their hands into their pockets - for the Emissaries <u>know</u> their weakness - (the weakness of the traitors) - I say the ones which would usurp the power and authority of the Emissaries shall learn well their lessons -- They shall come to <u>know</u> that there are NONE so foolish as the ones which THINK themself <u>wise</u> -- So be it I shall speak unto thee again and again - for I Am come that ye might come to know Me --
-

So be it - I AM - One of the Host --

Recorded by Sister Thedra of the Emerald Cross

Measure Not Anothers Stature by Thine Own

Mine Beloved Ones -- This day I would say unto thee - that Mine Servants are more blest than ALL the crowned heads of the Earth --

I say unto thee: "Mine Servants are MORE blest that ALL the crowned heads of Earth! -- For they shall wear the Crown of Glory! Theirs shall be the GREATER ---

So be it that I remember Mine Servants - and reward then in like measure for their service -- Nov let it be said - No man knoweth the measure of Mine Servants service - for they have not the greater vision -- So be it that I am come that these things be remembered -- And no man can measure anothers stature by his own -- So be it that I ask of thee - measure not anothers stature by thine own - for to attempt to do so is folly - for thou knowest not thine brother ---

I say thou knowest not thine self for that matter -- So be it that ye shall come to know -- I Am He which KNOWS - for I AM ONE with Mine Father Which hast sent ME ---

I AM

Recorded by Sister Thedra of the Emerald Cross

I Am Come That Mine Servants Be Lifted Up

Beloved Ones -- The time is come when ye shall bring forth great fruit - and it shall be GOOD -- It shall be of a variety which they have as yet not tasted -- I say: They have as yet not tasted of the fruit which ye shall bring forth - and it shall be "GOOD" and for this have I prepared thee ---

Let it be said that I shall raise up Mine Servants - and I shall exalt them over the KINGS of the Earth - for they shall do greater things than ALL the KINGS! ---

They shall be as ones exalted above all others which doth sit in high places of honor -- For Mine Servants shall be equal unto ME -- For they shall sit upon Mine right hand - and they shall bow down unto no man - or his puny opinions -- They shall know from whence their help cometh -- From whence they came -- And the CAUSE of their BEING -- So be it I Am come that Mine Servants be lifted up --

So be it and Selah ---

I AM Sananda

Recorded by Sister Thedra of the Emerald Cross

EL-O-HEIM
Soran - Speaks of the Candidate

Soran Speaking: - While I Am One of the Eloheim - I Am not of the Earth -- I Am not of woman born -- Neither am I of the nether world -- I say unto thee I AM of the ELOHEIM -- and I Am prepared to speak unto thee thusly ---

Be ye as one prepared to receive that which I say unto thee -- When it is given unto one to be lifted up - he has been obedient unto the law which is given unto them - (the Candidate) -- They walk as the Initiate -- They are not as the "infidel" - They betray not themself - They know that there is not any value in the work of the sinister force -- They have their hand out that their fellow man might be lifted up -- Yet they do not force it upon him -- He shows his hand - and exposes not himself unto then which would be unto him great torment ---

It is now come when it is necessary to walk silently and with dignity that ye expose not thineself unto the wonton ones -- I say let them seek thee out - and be ye as one prepared to give unto him as he is prepared to receive -- Let him seek first the Light - and no man shall take from him his right to see the Light -- Yet he shall prove himself -- And he shall find it necessary to walk the way set before him ---

I say the Candidate shall first prove himself - then he shall be as one lifted up -- For it is given unto him to first prepare himself for the Greater Part -- So be it and Selah ---

Let him which has ears to hear - hear that which I say unto thee - and let him profit thereby ---

I Am Come that they might be blest of Me and by Me ---

I AM Soran

Recorded by Sister Thedra of the Emerald Cross

Each Ones Responsibility Concerning Peace

Soran -- Mighty is the Word of God - and great the power thereof -- For this let it be said - that there is a mighty cry going out from all the Earth -- And the WORD hast gone out: Let there be Peace! Let there be Peace! -- And it shall be brot about thru the ones which are of a mind to follow in the footsteps of the Ones sent that it be established upon the Earth ---

It is said that there are Ones which have given of themself that there be Peace -- Yet they are not come that they transgress the law

91

- that they trespass upon a people - a nation -- They are come that the people be caused to awaken unto their true identity - their inheritance their own responsibility -- And it is said that Peace shall be found within them -- They shall have no hatred within themself -- They shall bear the responsibility given unto them -- Yet I say unto thee - each shall bear his own responsibility -- He shall walk upright and as one which has the mind to follow in the foot steps of the "Way Shower" -- Many have been sent that Peace be established within them - Yet they have not established it unto themself -- This is their own responsibility - their own part -- No man can do more than show the way - give them the law - and be unto them Brother -- I say they ask not of the Father for Peace that they be comforted - they ask of man -- It is as tho they were prepared to accept it - yet they are given a stone when they ask for bread -- It is said "Seek ye the Light - ask of the Father thine freedom" - Yet they know not the Father - they ask of their Idols - their own making -- They make of men heroes - and give unto them great glory -- I say they are as the ones crying for bread - knowing not from whence it cometh -- It is Mine part to give unto thee this Word - that they might receive it -- And it shall profit them which doth comprehend Mine Word -- For this hast it been spoken ---

I AM thine Brother of the Inner Temple -

Recorded by Sister Thedra of the Emerald Cross

The Plan is NOT 'Just a Piece of Paper!'

Beloved of Mine Being -- By the hand of the Almighty Father have I been sent that ye be brot out of bondage - that I might assist in the Great and Divine Plan -- I say it is for the GREAT AND MIGHTY

ASSEMBLY that the plan is carried thru - that it be carried to its completion - its fulfillment -- I tell thee that the Plan is far GREATER than an hast known - for the fullness hast not been revealed unto him -- He is not as yet prepared to comprehend -- For this he has not prepared himself -- He has not as yet overcome the selfish ways which is his ---

He has within himself that which holds him bound -- When it is said "Cut away thine legirons" - he has not comprehended the meaning thereof for he yet drags them with him -- Yet he asks for the fullness of the "Plan" - as tho it wast a piece of paper upon which he might behold some sort of Magic! -- I say the fullness his mind could not grasp! The fullness he could not comprehend - for it is great in scope - and perfect in its FIRST MAGNITUDE -- I say unto thee be ye as one prepared to receive it - for art thou not part of the Plan - art thou not Part??

I say "Behold the Work of the Plan - See it Work" - be ye one with it and comply with the law set forth -- And be ye glad for thine knowing the law -- For it is given unto thee to be One which has been given the LAW -- And it shall be fulfilled unto the letter -- So be it and Selah ----

Now ye shall remember thine Benefactors - and give unto them credit for that which THEY ARE - and give unto thine self credit for being a Son of God - for THOU ART YOU KNOW -- Has it not been said before?

Be ye blest this day --

For this have I come forth -- Therein is Mine

Word unto thee --

I AM -

Recorded by Sister Thedra of the Emerald Cross

On Peace

Beloved Ones;- This day let it be said that it is now come when there shall be wide-spread rumors of Peace; and there shall be no peace, for the peace which they ask is but appeasement. They have not found Peace, for it is not within them - it hast not been established within them. Yet they speak of others as though they had the power to give it or take it away.

I say: "Let Peace be established within thee, and no man can take it from thee". So be it I have spoken of Peace, yet they have not found peace. I have Peace, yet they have not accepted that which I offer them, for they sit in the seat of the scorner - the bigot - the hypocrite, and they speak of Me and about me, knowing Me not!

I say;- They deny Mine sayings; they but mumble that which is accredited unto Me. Yet I say THIS DAY, that they shall hear that which I say, for I shall SHOUT it from the Mountain tops!

I say;- "First seek ye the Light, and no man shall close it out".

I say;- No man shall deny thee. Let it be: "As thou prepare thyself, thou shall receive", so be it. I say;- "Seek ye the Light, and let Peace be established within thee, and no man shall take it from thee" - So be it.

I AM Sananda

Recorded by Sister Thedras of the Emerald Cross

The Way for Peace

-- While it is not yet come that they have found Peace; let it be said that peace only comes from within - no man finds it from without, for it is his own inheritance, and he pilfers not that of another.

I say; When they hold subject another, or impose upon another that which they have fortuned unto themself, they shall pay, for the law is clearly stated: "Ye shall not trespass upon the will of another". That implies any body of people; that implies the Countries - the Nations - and the single individuals.

Now, when a plan is established that each one has his own will granted unto him, he shall be solely responsible for the way in which he goes. Each country - nation, or individual, - each shall take upon itself/ himself, the responsibility for its being - or that which hast been brot into being.

While the nations of the Earth are battling for supremacy; I say, none are sufficient unto themself. Let it be understood that the time draws nigh when the way in which the greatest of all Nations has chosen to go shall be cut off - it shall be closed, and their progress shall cease; for it is not given unto the Light Forces to be still - without movement. They move with precision, knowing in which direction they go. Let it be said that aggression shall cease, and it shall not be tolerated! For this hast the Great Assembly raised its

95

Voice. Let it be said, that the <u>hostilities</u> <u>shall</u> <u>CEASE</u>! for this have I spoken out.

Yet there shall be great conflict ere it cease. Let it be, for this is the clearing away for Peace. I say; "They shall learn to <u>love one another</u>, and have Peace within them."

They shall learn from their suffering - so be it the law that they <u>learn</u>! so be it We shall not deny them that. When it is come that they have <u>learned</u>, WE shall then give unto them a hand, and it shall be for the GOOD OF ALL - So let it be.

I AM the One Sent that there be Peace

Light and Love established within them.

So be it I AM One of the Council

Recorded by Sister Thedra of the Emerald Cross

The Holy Words Shall Be Brought to Pass

Beloved Ones;- Hear ye this, and know ye that this is the Day for which thou hast waited. Let it be said that <u>this</u> is the DAY of the LORD, wherein all the Prophecies shall be fulfilled - wherein all the Holy Words shall be brot to pass. I say, this is the "Day of full-fillment" and for this hast thou waited; for this have We, the Mighty Council waited - yet not in vain.

I say unto thee: The Sacred Writ shall be remembered, and it shall be brot to remembrance in the days of fulfillment - for there shall be cause for remembrance. And when it is come that they are

96

brot face to face with their foolishness, they shall be reminded of their folly, and the Words which have been given unto them, that they might have WISDOM. I say; It hast been repeated many times; - "Look ye unto the Father for thine sustenance, and know ye that he is the Giver of Life - He is the Cause of thine Being". And He gives and He takes without revenge. So be it that He hast given into thee graciously and lovingly, - and then I see them turn their face from Him and seek in dark places for wisdom!

Wherein have they found their freedom? surely not in the world of men!! Wherein have they found Peace? surely not within the "World of Men"!

I say: I come not to bring peace; yet I come that they might know from whence cometh their peace. Let it be established within them, and no man can then take it from them.

So be it I have repeated it many times, yet there is no peace within them which cry Peace! Peace! Peace! They but make a mockery of the "WORD", and at no time shall they find it without - they shall establish it within themself, then they shall be as ones prepared for the "Greater Part". Let it be.

I AM Sananda

Recorded by Sister Thedra of the Emerald Cross

Strength

Beloved of Mine Being;- Let this be written for them which will that they might read, that they might know that which I say. While they have not the ears to hear that which I say, let it be written that they

97

might read, that they might have the knowledge that there is a "PLAN", and that they are not the creators of it. I say, they run hither and yon, asking of man and his opinion, that they might find consolation in their own. And it is for this that I speak out at this time. When it is given into man to know his Source, he shall at no time ask of another 'his opinion', for he shall have the knowledge of all things what-so-ever - he shall no longer ask of others his opinion about anything, for he shall KNOW - and for a surety!

I say: When he hast become unbound, he shall know! and be as one wise!

Yet it is given unto man as a whole to seek for Light, and he knows not whither to go that he might find it. He hast neither the mind or the will to search out the Light; to seek out the Light that he finds his way. I say, it is given unto them to weary of the search; they falter near the attainment; they heed not the admonition: "COME".

I say, they weary and fall by the way. Hear ye that which I say, and know ye that there are many prepared to assist, yet they have their hands above thine head; They are not thine servants; They give unto thee work which shall be done, and at no time shall it be more than ye can bear. They give generously of themself that ye be strengthened in thine weak parts, and that ye be about the Father's business. So be it that I am One which hast given of Mineself that ye be spared this day - that ye be as ones prepared, that ye be kept for this day. Now it is given unto Me to know that which lies before thee, and I speak wisely and with compassion.

Let it be written, that the time draws nigh when the floods shall rage; the fires shall take many forms, and it shall lay waste the wonderlands of the world. It shall leave behind it the blackness of destruction and desolation; it shall sweep the lands wherein there is great and marvelous forests; it shall be as ye have not seen!

Let it be written that: the water shall be of no avail, for the waters shall not be unto them comfort; it too shall be as one gone mad; it too shall be as ye have not known, for the lakes shall dry; the rivers shall change their course - they shall overflow their banks; the dams shall break. And I say unto thee: They shall be as ones entrapt, distraught, and there shall be great loss of property, and many shall lose their forms of flesh.

Now for this have We said: "Prepare thineself". Fear YE NOT! and seek no hiding place, for there is no hiding place. I say, "Seek ye the Light", let Peace fill thine heart, and know ye that ye are NOT alone.

So be it I am One which stands by to give assistance - be ye as ones prepared to receive it, for it is proffered in Love and Mercy, and with Wisdom. Be ye blest of Mine Presence.

I AM thine Older Brother and thine Sibor,

Sanat Kumara

Recorded by Sister Thedra of the Emerald Cross

Ye Walk Not Alone

Sanat Kumara speaking:- With the Love and Compassion which is Mine, I bow before the Light which I serve, and I place within thine hand Mine hand, that ye might take it - that ye might have Mine assistance, that ye might know that ye walk not alone.

So be it that I am One of the Mighty Council, and at no time, shall WE betray Our trust - neither shall We forget that which hast been said unto thee.

Let it be said this day, that the Way is opened for thine return unto thine abiding place. I say, ye shall return unto thine Source and receive thine Inheritance in full.

Now let it be said; Not all shall accept the Gift of comprehension; not all shall accept the Gift which has been given for their acceptance, - they have but to prepare themself for to receive it.

It is said: "Cut away thine legirons, ye cannot bring them into this place", for therein is wisdom.

When it is said: "Prepare thine self" it is little understood by man! for to prepare thineself is to be able to receive the Greater Part; and it is the law: The "Cup" shall first be emptied out - cleansed, that it be filled with the First Substance, that of Light Substance, which is the first and pure Substance. This is the turning away from the old - the putting on the NEW; the shedding of the old garment - taking up the new, the bright and shining Armor of God. The Light is not tarnished, it is pure, shining and dazzling to behold!!

I say unto thee: Place thine hand in Mine; accept that which We offer unto thee, and be ye as one free forever - for this have I revealed Mineself unto thee.

Blest are they which know Me, for I am He which is known as Sanat Kumara

Recorded by Sister Thedra of the Emerald Cross

These Shall be the "Just"

-- Mine Beloved;- The time cometh when thine lands shall bring forth no vegetation; no place where they might turn for relief.

While it is said that they have not the comprehension to know - the eyes to see, they have not been unto themself true, - for where shall they escape? I say, there is NO escape! They shall be inheritors of their desolation, for they shall lay waste the land, and they shall inherit their desolation. So be it and Selah.

Let it be said, that they shall cry for relief, and great shall be their torment.

So be it that we of "The Council" have provided a way for the Just and Obedient. I say: The Law is just, and all who abide thereby shall be called "JUST", and they shall be spared the torment which the unjust shall endure. I say: "As they have sown so shall they reap" - so be it the law, and the law is JUST. For this is it written that: "They shall be warned".

Let them which have ears to hear; them which have a mind to learn, let them learn. So be it I have spoken, that they be spared. So let it Be.

I AM

Recorded by Sister Thedra of the Emerald Cross

Sananda Answers "Them"

Beloved Ones;- This is Mine time, and I say unto thee: Hold thine head high, and be ye as Mine Servant, and let not the foul winds blow into thine dwelling place, for I say unto thee: Them which strut themself, and they which bear false witness of Mine Servants, shall be brot to account for their folly. So be it I see them running hither and yon, and being unto themself great comfort. I say, they comfort themself, and it is given unto them to be boastful as well as deceitful. So be it that I am come that there be Light, - and it is given into few to stand steadfast and seek the greater part. They are content to accept the praise and glory of men. Yet unto them I say: "Be ye not puffed up, for the day cometh when ye shall cry for assistance!" So be it I know, for the Law is just.

I ask only obedience unto the Law, and none maketh a mockery of Mine Words, unknown, for all things are known within the place wherein I am. I am not mocked for I say unto them;- The day cometh when I shall go out, and I shall walk amongst them as One unknown; and they shall not have the comprehension to know Me. For I am not to be put aside, neither am I to be put into a closet, - I say, there is NO hiding the LIGHT which I AM. And too I say: WOE unto any man which deny Me, for I say, I am Sent of Mine Father that there be Light, and for this hast He sent Me. So be it and Selah.

I have spoken unto the foolish which <u>THINK</u> themself wise. So let it be.

I AM Sananda

Recorded by Sister Thedra of the Emerald Cross

TRANSCRIPTS OF THE MASTERS

Introduction to The Transcripts

In 1955 these transcripts were released for the first time.

Many hands, many workers in the light assisted in their preparation.

Unfortunately, this material was recently plagiarized and published in a book titled THE BROTHERHOOD OF THE SEVEN RAYS--

SECRETS OF THE ANDES. It was done without authority, without permission of the Brotherhood of the Seven Rays.

Once more they are being sent out by Divine command through the efforts of Sister Thedra, who was present at the original sessions. They are unedited and in their original form.

As is true of all material coming through this channel, the transcripts are sent upon request and on a love offering basis.

This is necessary because there is no earthly sponsor.

BROTHER N.

Concerning These Transcripts

Now ye shall give unto them which read that part (these transcripts), this word. And ye shall say unto them in my name that there are none so sad as the one which betrays himself, or his trust. So be it and Selah.

Now ye shall go into the place there in there are the ones which have given unto this part of these transcripts. (*)

And ye shall find therein the complete transcripts which have been recorded from the hand of one called Sananda, and the one herein given so be it that this part of the plan has been kept as a separate account, for it is apart from that of thy own work.

I am now speaking unto thee, my Sister Thedra, of the Emerald Cross, and ye are the one which I have appointed unto this office; and ye shall now place this, my testimony, within this book of transcripts.

And was it not said that there are none so sad which betrays himself: so it is a truth indeed.

And when these transcripts were spoken there was but one purpose--which they knew not------.

And they were as ones which had within their hand the key to the gate--yet they chose to go the long way round, for they have gone the back way--and they have not given credit where credit is due; and for this we here at this council table do cut them off without our aid.

I say they which do pilfer and distort the words of the SONS OF GOD are a stench within our nostrils; and they have been unto us offensive.

And I say they are cut off--until they have been sufficiently prepared to enter into the place where in they may be groomed for the part which shall be given unto them; and they shall EARN the right to call themself "SIBORS'--they are as yet not sibets! (**)

For they have not learned the first lesson--that of LOVE and RESPECT one for the other--and obedience unto the LAW. And this is not of my ownself that they are cut off: I say they have cut themself off, and I am sad, so be it and Selah.

Ye shall now add this unto the record, and I shall set my seal unto it--and ye shall be within the law to say that ye were within the place where in I am for a period of time and I have spoken unto thee on this subject of wonton which is rebelliousness--and which is not of the Father.

For when a candidate for the GREAT LEARNING presents himself he is divested of all his wonton and willfulness; he stands as one without any opinion--he gives credit where credit is due--so be it the better part of wisdom.

I have spoken and I am finished. Sananda, known unto them as Jesus Christ, Amen, so be it.

(*) These Masters which are speaking in these transcripts.

(**) Sibor--an all-wise, all-knowing one. One illumined of God the Father--   THE SOURCE OF ALL KNOWLEDGE.

A sibet is a candidate for such revelation--one who has prepared himself and presented himself as a candidate for the GREAT LEARNING, or ILLUMINATION.

106

Sanat Kumara Speaking
(Received 2/19/56)

Aramu-u-u-u-u, Aram-u-u, Aramu-u-u, Aramu, Aramu, Aramu, Aramu, Ara-a-a-a-aum, A-a-a-um, Aum,

Beloved of my bosom, and beloved of my being, all space is vibrant with love, harmony, and peace, as directed by many men from many spheres. The light of their love is ever growing into a great flame that shall consume all lust, greed, hatred, malice, and shall sweep over the Earth as a great tidal wave. Long ago, as I witnessed a great Star that appeared in the East, this was the sign unto man of Earth that redemption draweth nigh, that salvation was present. No soul, no matter how degraded, shall be denied admittance to the great school of life. This is the time when truly the lion shall lie down with the lamb.

On the Earth there has been the great confusion of man's mind that has caused the turmoil and even the seas to boil in hatred themselves; but He who came to prove that the troubled waters can be calmed and stilled, the fury of the night winds can be hushed by the raising of one hand, not the raising of a hand to slay and to curse, but the raising of a hand in loving benediction--and all the elements that are commanded and should be commanded by man--for the Father placed the Earth and all celestial bodies in the heavens. They are created out of spiraling primordial matter for man. Man was to be the god of physical form: man, the highest expression of Deity known in the entire Omniverse.

Oh, man! realize that you are the highest form of Deity anywhere in the Omniverse! There is nothing beyond you. And in this you are grand; and in this you are the lowest. You are the lowest because you <u>know</u> and the other life forms do not know. Therefore, you must be their brother and you must be their servant, because you know. You know!

There is life and intelligence in all forms, as ancient man knew. Man alone is not the only thinking being. Man knows and the others do not, but they think nevertheless. Every element, every mineral-- all forms--have inherent intelligence, and it is up to man as their keeper and as their elder brother, even as Sananda is our Elder Brother. You are the elder brother of these forms, innumerable forms throughout the Omniverse. It is up to you to raise them to ever higher and higher evolution as they, along with man--man who is their god-- progress up the worlds to infinite grandeur, to Infinite Light.

Oh, the beauty of the age that now approaches! when all doubts, when all fears shall be rolled away as a great scroll! And there shall be a great thundering! The heavens are torn asunder! And then man views himself; man looks into the mirror of knowing. No longer is there confusion. Man accepts the MANTLE OF GOLD. Man accepts the scepter of his godhood so that no longer may his progression up the stars be hindered by the darkness of ignorance and superstition.

Beloved of my being, know this, and in knowing it there must of necessity be sadness; and yet there must be gladness for the beauty that it shall bring.

But now for a moment I do speak on that which impends, that which is forthcoming. Yes, there can be atomic detonations; there can be cosmic ray bombardments, but these are the effects. What is the cause? The cause of the destruction that shall come upon the Earth is from man's own thinking.

Since the time when the Sons of God came in unto the daughters of man and animal-men appeared upon the Earth he has been striving from beasthood back to angelhood. But faulty thinking shall new break forth as the elements refuse to be regarded as they have been for millennia upon the Earth. The elements! they are intelligent life! They are part of the INFINITE ONE, and because they are part of the INFINITE ONE they will not respond to man's negative thinking any longer. And they will rebel, causing great tidal waves and great winds! Millions shall perish! yea millions! They shall be reborn anew on other worlds appropriate to their level of progression. And because of the remnant that must remain, the Earth is purified and raised to a new vibration.

Very soon, beloved of my being, the winds shall howl, sooner than we can realize. It is already upon us, for I have witnessed it in the plane which is just above that of physical expression upon the Earth, and that means that if it descends one more plane it shall find reality. And that which you knew must come on a December not too many months ago shall find its reality, for it is in the plane ready to descend into form and motion upon the Earth.

The fields and the great cities shall be desolate without inhabitant. Can you imagine a great city such as London, New York, Paris, where millions of men and women love, work, and play? Can you imagine a more desolate scene than a city of millions without inhabitant? It is like suddenly the Universe has been deprived of men, for the joy of the CREATOR is in HIS highest expression--

man. Without man He is without love. Even though man can be HIS greatest hurt, man also can raise HIM to the greatest aspiration. For without man even the INFINITE ONE cannot progress, for why would we limit HIM? If man can progress cannot He progress also? Cannot HE through HIS own creation find new thrills in love?

Oh, man of Earth! if you knew the love that descends to you from spheres innumerable, from minds inviolate! If you would listen you would know. There can be nothing but beauty. From all the catastrophe that shall come only the vision of a beautiful rose shall remain, for man steps forth in a purified light of his own creation.

The forces of the Black Dragon--they can deafen the ears of man to the music of the spheres, to the melodies, the angelic hosts, but yet they have not found power to still the celestial movements for, no matter how powerful their armies, the Moon will still remain to meet the dawn of a new day. And they have not yet learned how to still the melodic song of the brook nor can they in their attainments reach the heights that the eagle can reach in his soaring upward, ever upward, as a great prayer that rises from the Earth toward the Infinite Throne, for the eagle is master of the Earth above all of them.

Remember the beauty of Earth is in the creation that you stand upon, that you derive your nourishment from. It is like the bosom of our Father, where we rest our head to regain strength. It is our mother and yet it is our father. The Earth is a beautiful world, vastly more beautiful than some of its neighbors. I have always loved the Earth beyond all other creations, for I see within it a melody that has not yet escaped into the ethers. I see it crying as one bound. But it shall not be deprived its celestial song much longer!

No, I say that the Black Dragon, with all its negative force, has not been able to take away one iota from the beauty of the creation. Never has this dark force been able to really take away the beauty of that which is truly of the INFINITE ONE. This force has not been able to deny the brook or the world the twilight song. Yea, if they could they would deprive the gentleness of night, the twilight song. I say now is the time when the dusty feet of gods shall become the dust that swirls about their ugly forms. Idle rust, rust must be! Oh, man! hear this proclamation that comes upon the face of the Earth: idle rust rust must be! Brazen brass the Earth must be!

It is truly recorded in the greatest archives of akasha that God did truly provide and man divided. That is the motto of Earth. Man must come back from the multitudinous sins to the ONE, for it is not in complexity that we find the Father. It is in simplicity that we find Him. Yes, indeed! idle rust rust must be; brazen brass brass must be. Now man standing alone with only the light between him and the Father sufficing for all enlightenment of the stars.

As you serve, remember each and every one of your fellow-men is deity. Think of each one that you meet each day not as this man or that woman or this child or that child, but that each one that comes before you is the Father in essence. If you would think on Earth of each one as part of the Father, with due respect in that degree, then the Earth's problems would dissolve instantly.

And now the hungry multitudes of Earth are crying; they're crying for a Sananda that can once again give them the loaves and fishes, who, from a small paltry substance, can feed them and satisfy their great hunger. They are crying now for the waters of life, for the manna of wisdom. And I say that it is written--it is an edict from the

HIGHEST ONE HIMSELF-- that this shall be done, for HE has commanded: "These are my children; they must be led back to my bosom and they must be fed my substance."

We who hold the Earth in our hand were given her to develop, to cherish, and to bring to fruition. We now see that the harvest shall be ample and the storehouse of the Father will be full for the migration to new grandeur of being.

Beloved of my being, I would give you a divine commandment for the time immediately ahead: Oh, feed the sheep of Sananda! Give, where it is required. Give not of your past glories but give them that which the soul needs. Tell them, tell them I say, that there shall be catastrophe! Prepare them for that. But tell them out of this shall come the greater light,--tell them that, yes, through the catastrophe that comes upon the Earth, for the night cometh when no man can work, and the night is now here-the doubt of catastrophe and disaster and despair. And the flood gates and the winds shall wash and blow away all the old--the old. It was the spawn of darkness; for it can be endured by all men if they know beyond is rainbow's end, the golden promise of godhood and oneness with our Father.

Beloved ones, if you only knew upon worlds without number in space--stars of great majesty and beauty that appear like great beautiful radiant gems in the black velvet of the Omniverse--the millions of souls that are crying out, and their voices ring out in appeal of peace toward the Earth. If men were aware of such love and such affection and such direction the problems of Earth would not be problems at all.

Therefore it is your duty to bring them this message which is a two-fold message: a warning, a warning to prepare for that which shall come in the waves and the winds; and it is a message secondarily that there are those who care, who are acting as the emissaries of the INFINITE ONE. Tell them they are loved. Tell them that they shall be guided as they ask to be guided: "Ask, and ye shall receive; knock, and it shall be opened unto you."

They shall be caught up. They shall be where the eagles gather. They shall not be found wanting. Tell them that their Father has heard them. Their Father is ever gracious and ever loving to His children.

Once again, coming from the Earth Planet shall be the radiant thoughts of love as they adore HIM, their CREATOR, for once again the discordant planet in this Solar System will no longer be the "Lost Chord", but will join with the other eleven in the perfect melody.

I am he who is only--who is only as great as the smallest particle of sand on the Earth and is only as low as the highest mountain top. I have known countless existences upon this beloved planet: To know now the sweet essence of the breeze and the cedars of Lebanon, the aspen of America; to feel the gentle waters caressing the many shores on the world; to know the harmony as the beautiful plant life of the planet responds to the minds of man.

On Earth the great kingdoms that would serve man: the mineral, the vegetable, the animal life--it is in a state of chaos; because that which was created to be its master is not a master at all. The mineral life, the vegetable life, the animal life finds that its god, its master, is a drunken master who reels to and fro in his folly. That is why they now rebel against the drunken master. But on other worlds--on other worlds they respond and they caress their master, and the result is a great vibrant life-giving essence that is beyond comprehension, that is beyond my power to describe to you.

Has not the man often wished to go back to the security, the warmth of the mother? I say it is equally true of man for the Father. Man of Earth knows where he must go but he cannot always find the way. Therefore, beloved of my being, the coming times directly ahead of you all point that way to Him; for that shall be your shibboleth of spirit. That shall be. I shall be!

I have spoken to you this evening from out of the smallest of the creation on Earth and out of the largest: the small and the large being one in HIM.

And the cry from all over the Omniverse, from all the innumerable star systems and worlds, coning down from HIM-- HIM! Aramu! Aramu! The cry is: "Oh, children of Earth, come home! Come home again! Come home again!! You have been so long absent from our hearts. Come home and fill the emptiness of our beings. Come home! We are awaiting thee. We are awaiting thee." Aramu.

Oh, Father of us all, lift us up on thy eternal wings and present us pure in thy light. Oh, Father! Father of us all!

Peace to you from all Creation. Sanat Kumara, My peace to you.

Sanat Kumara Speaking
(Received 3/4/56)

A-a-a-a-aum-m-m. Beloved of my being, light from the Eternal Mind, I have asked to speak with you again this day because for me it is the time of the great initiation and, in a smaller sense, it is the time of your great initiation to another place of consciousness.

It was a time long ago that I was called to the Earth to perform a certain mission to the children of men. And now the time has come for me to return to Venus to be by her side as she enters the great initiation. Therefore, I did desire to speak with you today.

This day upon the holy Sea of Galilee their armies clash by night. It is the beginning of the end and the end of the beginning, as it was prophesied of old, for today the long strife that has taken place in the "unholy" Holy Land has reached an apex, a culmination point-- the armies of Egypt and Syria and the armies of Israel. This is a very significant happening, as my beloved Brother, Master K. H., has told you many times.

This is the place to watch in the world, the place that is the spark that shall ignite the approach of He whom we await; and do we not wait upon Him with exceeding patience and pleasure to dwell upon?

This is the lesson that we all must learn, not once but many many times, over and over again, in worlds of great magnificent splendor as well as in worlds that are veiled and worlds that are dark in culture and development. How many times have we learned this lesson? Many, many millions of times; and we will always continue to learn, for, take away curiosity and take away the thrill of living and seeking

115

and man could not exist. There would not even be a creation. So we shall never reach the end of that road. We shall always seek. If it is not countries or lands and peoples, then it shall be worlds, or suns, or systems, or galaxies, or super-galaxies, and beyond that we shall know pleasure in the realms of light themselves, each one adding its own vibration and its own light.

The great law--one of them--is that in order to receive we must give, for, like the giant water basin, it can receive the heavenly rains until it chokes and swells and runs over, but it must run over, giving of its abundance to the dry parched ground beneath it. If it does not, then it bursts and can contain no more. But if it does give of its abundance, then when the great rains come again from heaven, it will be replenished all the more and again can give as the hungry earth drinks it in every drop and waits for the great water vessel to give of its abundance.

It was decreed long ago that I should come to Earth to assist--to assist our Elder Brother, Sananda, who rules this System, and to assist all our beloved brothers and sisters upon the Earth Planet. But I was at a certain time to return once again to my own Venus, the planet which has been given to me as my ward. Therefore I had to give whatever I had in abundance to my Earth children, to my Earth brethren. Now that I have done that--and I say it without any feelings of egotism--that I have fulfilled this task, now I shall receive of the latter rains that will come. Only those vessels that have...receive of the latter rain.

Let me go back in time, just a short time, to when you were tried-- which centered around the very fateful day of December twenty-first--a year not far gone. This was a time when it was to be determined if you could give of your abundance, and you did give of it. You gave so well that the water vessel almost became dry in the giving. Then the latter rains did come and you were filled once again. So ever be it a process in our development through many millennia. We give and we receive; but every time that we receive we receive more. The water vessel is not a stationary permanent thing. It becomes ever larger, ever more shapely, ever more perfect in the eyes of the Father. From a crude clay vessel it becomes a vessel like unto a gem of finely cut crystal.

The mentors that have been with you in the past, really just a few short weeks, that have given certain information, small as it was, and not even a small fraction of what really remains, but they gave what they did know, as I must give now that I return to Venus.

But our entire Solar System, beloved ones, is now coming into the great initiation, for it is true that we are now heading directly for the Super-sun which governs our Galaxy, the Super-sun around which countless island universes perpetually move and have existence. Our System is heading for the center of this activity and this increased rate of vibration will profoundly affect every thing in our System; whether it be mental, physical, or spiritual it will not escape the change in the new vibration of energy that is coming. We are now on the outskirts of this great initiation. But every second that ticks of every day we are heading closer and closer to its center and fulfillment.

Therefore I would stand with Venus at this time. That is why Sananda returns to the Earth: because always the great Master of a solar system incarnates and gives aid to the planet which is lowest in progression in that system, and also because He is the spirit of the

Earth, which He achieved that position in His incarnation as the teacher, Buddha. Buddha was for the Earth, but the Christ is for the System.

Let us take as an example two men. Both have committed the same error exactly in all its details. Each one has done the same thing. But can we condemn each man equally? No, we cannot condemn either man. But let us look into the cause of things. To sum up all the difficulties that the Red Star Earth experiences for the millennia that I have been here, I could sum it up in just a few words. On the Earth man only looks to effect, and never to cause. Once he looks into the heart of things he will find that it is the heart of the Father Himself; then from there all the rays of creation proceed out from Him. He will never find it by looking at the rays alone. He cannot trace it from effect to cause. It must be from cause to effect. So let us look not at the effect which is what each man has done but let us look at the cause.

Let us take one man. We find that he has done this thing through ignorance of the law. The other man had knowledge of the law. It is said in your world that ignorance of the law is no excuse, but in the Father's realm ignorance of the law is an excuse. But once we have learned the law, if we falter and make error, then we are indeed in a different category than those who through ignorance perform the same thing. You see, the sin or error is not in stepping into the hole in the ground, but the error is in stepping in it twice, once we know it is not the thing to do.

Therefore, I give this example to show you the condition that the Earth is in at the present time. The Earth has had many civilizations and, when one has gone to the bottomless pit, man rises in his

118

cultural development and again builds a great and glorious civilization with great scientific and technical advance. But again the civilization drops to the bottomless pit. There is the error of the Earth, for on Venus there has never been a destruction of a civilization. It has occurred on the planet you know as Kars twice. But how many hundreds of times has it taken place on the earth!

Man must learn to apply knowledge once he has attained to it. You are now in the process of developing your physical forms. If you develop them and attain it, yet you do not apply what you have learned, you will soon lose what you have attained. In fact, you perhaps would be in worse condition than you were before you started.

So man on Earth must learn; apply the knowledge that he has learned in constructive channels. Therefore, once we have asked, because the father has said if we ask we shall receive--once we have asked and have received, the law is: we must apply what we have received, and then we must give what we have received. I have received much during my mentoring on Earth, which now I go to give of myself to my own, to my own home, to my own people; but the Earth shall always be close to my heart.

And now we enter this great period of initiation. The skies of Earth will become fantastic! Through many prophecies that have come to you through various members of your group and from other people working throughout the world, you feel that you have an insight into what shall take place; and yet I say verily that pen has not recorded nor voice uttered that which shall become a great sign and display in the skies of Earth, for the elements themselves will have control for a short period of time. There will be great great rainstorms and floods. You have heard how it raided forty days and nights. That is nothing compared to what it will rain. Perhaps it would be forty months. The entire face of the Earth shall change. It will not be recognized any more at all. All geographies and maps will become obsolete in each case.

Strange creatures shall appear from the depths of the oceans to the wonderment and bewilderment of men, creatures many many times larger than the largest ocean liners! There shall be plagues and famines! Beasts and creatures unknown shall appear!

When the Earth is about ready to become a sun, --not like the Sun of your System, --but it shall be surrounded by a golden corona. It is stepping into a higher rate of vibration. It will become a sun; but that which it is is not known in your system of astronomy because it has never been viewed by your astronomers. You are going from a three dimensional to a fourth dimensional world. No longer will those in this dimension be able to even see you or your world. This must necessarily take place as you pass through the heart of the great cosmic cloud.

And then shall the prophecies, as recorded by Joel and many of the others, come true: when the Sun shall turn blood red and the Moon shall be red as the ruby, and the day shall be gone and it shall be dark upon the Earth for a period of two weeks. There shall be much confusion. And the oxygen will be reduced upon the Earth for a short period, followed by periods of great moisture, alternating-- baking heat and parched areas alternating with great moisture. Almost everything upon the face of the Earth will be destroyed.

When is this time coming? We are now in it. Each day it grows in intensity. More of your craft that fly in the air are coming down. Every day you hear of it. More tornados! More floods! The great snows in Europe this winter--now they are melting, to deposit Europe in a great flood. The Polar caps melting more each day! The water levels rising!

The governments of the world are in panic, yet they do not show it outwardly. Beneficial bacteria upon the Earth which you depend upon--your very existence-- upon these little creatures, are dying at a rapid rate, so that you will be exposed more and more to that which is detrimental to your systems.

All would end upon the Earth two years from today--all would be dead upon the face of the Earth if it were not for the fact that some will be able to raise their vibration to the new level. But remember, as you see that which decays and dies and disintegrates before your eyes, it is because all is being made new. Rejoice in-- that you see these things, for it is your salvation which draweth nigh. It is not your doom. And therefore you must tell your fellow-man that yes, the catastrophes come, but it is your salvation. Rejoice! for the old passes away! Sic mundi gloria transit! "So passeth the glory of this world!"

If man can release the old, then he shall glimpse a more glorious new. Those who cannot release the old will have to start over at the very beginning. They shall place their soul progression back several million years, and once again will have to come up through various forms of cave man through thousands of years, even millions, until they develop to this very stage again. And then they shall have the chance once again to accept the new and, if they cannot accept the new then, they will go back once again millions of years.

This, beloved ones, is not retrogression as it would appear. It is retrogression in the physical, yet it is progression from the standpoint of spiritual evolvement, for in the Father's realm there is no retrogression--only continual expanding grandeur.

Oh, so that we might find ourselves worthy to be and pass through the great initiation! For whether a being or a man or a spirit or a soul entity, whether he commands a planet or a solar system or only his own little family, he never knows if he will stand the fire, the test of fire of a great initiation.

So remember, apply that which we have learned and give gladly that which we have received. As you travel and as you converse in the times ahead allotted for each one of us, think not what you shall take with you or what shall be in your purse or what you shall wear. Think not on these things because the Father will provide. Accept that and it shall be done unto you, for verily you have accepted a trust and you have accepted a mission; and the Father will supply from His abundant storehouse unto you in that you serve well.

So this is not a time of a test as it was one December; no, it is not a test. It is time of giving and applying. And that is exactly what I go to do now myself. It is not the clarion call or the order which is given to you alone, but it is the order of the day now as we enter into this new phase for the Planet Earth, and indeed our whole System.

Work, beloved ones, for the night cometh shortly when no man can work! work for the night cometh! Literally and figuratively. Tell your fellow-man when he asks: "We do not know what to believe. Some say catastrophe shall come upon us. They claim the end of the world is here. Others claim, 'be not afraid; we through our own scientific developments--we are masters of the creation--we can do this or that.'" Man is seeking. His heart is hungrier than it has ever been before because he feels the pew vibrations.

Is it not true, dear ones, that a hungry man is even more hungry when he smells food? Even as Sananda was tempted in the desert when He was fasting, is not a man who is fasting, --is he not more susceptible to temptation of savory morsels of food?

So man smells this food, this new vibration, and he is ever more hungry. It has whetted his appetite for things of spirit. Therefore when he is confused as he is and he says, "Brother, where shall I find the greatest meal which shall give me the most satisfaction for development of my spirit?" you shall say: "Yes, those who say catastrophe comes are true; they speak with truth; but the Earth will not end. It shall become new, as it is written. It does not say the world will end. It says there shall be a 'new heaven and a new earth,' not a new Earth through the destruction of the old, but a new Earth--the old made new."

So tell them the words that the Elder Brother wishes you to feed His flock with. It is the way of the Father, I say, unto you. Catastrophe comes so that man might learn from the experience. But only the great and beautiful and good shall be inherited from it. Out of it mankind shall arise phoenix-like unto his own golden glory.

How often we look upon the Earth, knowing within our hearts as we look upon each small and pitiful creation and creature, that here stands a god if he would only realize it--apply his godhood. For a true god sits not on a throne in inactivity while the masses come before him adoring him. That is not godhood as some on Earth would think, but godhood is enthronement, yes, but a god of action who enters the being of each one of his creation; fill then with life and majesty and grandeur.

God wishes man--man that He created to rule over His celestial worlds. He wishes each man to take charge of His worlds. Recognize that each one of your fellow-men that passes you during the routine of the day--recognize him as a potential god. For some day, beloved ones, each one, no matter whether they are in your institutions of correction, whether they have gone to your gas chambers, or to the Haman's noose, some day that soul will command a planet, and then a system and a galaxy. We are all on the road to that legacy. And the clarion call is: "Come home Earth!" as I have said, "Come home to the emptiness of our beings!"

When each man can feel, actually feel the love and friendship from another man from all creation, then the lion shall lie down with the lamb, as it is written, when all thought is harmonious. For we are all part of one ETERNAL MIND and, to come back into that MIND, we must all join our spirits together.

(Sanat Kumara Speaking)

(Archangel Michael Speaking)

(Joseph of Arimathea Speaking)

Do not become weary from the routine of the day. Always keep the goal before you, not the eternal goal, for there is no eternal goal, but keep the goal of the moment which shall be an eternal goal, in & sense. Keep it before you ever shining like a great golden sun. Turn not your face from its radiance or its warmth. Stay within it. Let it enshroud you in its warmth. Go where the Father doth lead. Do what the Father feels is best for you, and the service you render.

For this is the time that you have died countless times over, for which you have been crucified, whether you were a man or a man on a throne. Accept now your graduation, and prepare for the great initiation. Sanat Kumara.

Archangel Michael Speaking

Ave! Ave! Realize that you are never alone. Realize that it would be impossible for you to be alone. You are attached for eternity to the brotherhood of service.

The Golden Helmeted Ones surround the Earth ever more as we enter into the greet initiation. We are plunging ever deeper into that which shall be our destruction and yet it shall be our salvation, even as He who went to the cross of pain. It was His destruction and yet it was his glorious Transfiguration.

May we be worthy, beloved ones, may we be worthy of the Cross. Michael of the Sun.

Joseph of Arimathea Speaking

Greetings in the light of the Cross. This is thy brother, Joseph. I was not invited to speak, and yet I add my words to those of our teacher, Sanat Kumara, our beloved Sanat Kumara, who now leaves us. And yet we have known of his spirit and his substance. Therefore he can never be completely gone from us forever and ever.

But I wish to say to you: the Grail, remember the Grail. It is shining and glowing and beckoning even as it was to you long centuries ago when we held it within our hands. It is the symbol, the little clay Cup--the little clay Cup of earth--that symbolizes the Earth, that shall shortly be filled to overflowing, not with the blood of a deceased savior but with the manna from the Father--the manna of true cosmic wisdom and understanding.

Beloved ones, receive, apply, and give freely. And soon we shall stand together, and we shall see the Grail returned to the Earth in the firmament. So be it!

Archangel Uriel Speaking
(Received 2/12/56)

Beloved of my knowings. On the emanations from Deity and the emanations of Deity, my love to you.

Before the memory of man recounteth this tale, we beings known to mortal man as archangels were the only living thought in a certain vast limitless part of the Father's realm. We journeyed like the legions of Caesar, yet without weapon, without weapon of stone or steel, but with weapon as a double-edged sword. Only Truth could exist in this vast limitless ocean that you would fain call space. Yet it is not space. It is a breathing, living creature of such beauty and magnificence that if mortal man could view it he would cease to exist in form and in thought.

126

We were called out of the emanations of Deity because we were to know service and substance thereof. We came not at a great trumpet's call but because in this great void would appear shortly worlds and millions of the Father's creation. So-called angelic hosts of faraway worlds, galaxies, systems and heavens, passed ever forward in and out cleansing and purifying with waves of violet haze and purple clouds.

Once we viewed a great spiraling ball of fire circling ever in its great elliptical orbit, finally coming to rest in a certain position beyond the great orb you know as the Sun, for this was an intruder; this was an intruding world that surrounded the Sun, because under the dazzling corona of this orb our worlds existed, not looking into blue of sky but looking into the gold of Sun, looking into the dazzling radiance of gold. There is more reality under the light of the Sun than there is in the blue of the sky in which the planetary worlds exist and know their movements.

We had known life on the Sun before the worlds came. Then the Earth--one of the newest members of the System--the child that was added, even as Judas Iscariot was added as Twelve--the Earth was added as twelfth planet, the last of the worlds. They did not arrive according to their position from or to the Sun.

And then after countless ages we watched this red ball of fire turn black as the fires diminished; and then we watched it turn brown, and the rains came for thousands of years,--for millions of years it rained, if you can but fathom it! Then the planet became green and brought forth all manner of flesh, flying creatures; and the creatures of the deep brought forth after their own kind; and the

Earth was ready to receive the seed of man--angel-man. We have watched this procession down countless millions of years.

And now out of the past there is a sounding, the sounding of a silver trumpet. When the Beloved Teacher, who is Lord in this Solar System, came to Earth, the heavenly hosts rejoiced, even as it is written they rejoiced on that night when He arrived. And above was the sign of the night: the Blue-White Star that came and embraced the Earth in its radiance and in its love from the angelic hosts afar.

Oh, man of Earth! you speak of the things of heaven! yet you understand not even the things of Earth! Indeed heaven is all about you! You have but to look up from your daily routines, from your daily misgivings and your waywardness, and your lusts and your greed, to realize that heaven is all about you in ever expanding grandeur.

And now after all this time, for millions of years of rain, as we think on these things, the time that man has been on Earth is as but a moment. And yet again the rain shall come and purify, the rains that it is truly written of shall be the "latter rain, "--the "latter rain," --but first the winds. Going back through the stages of the planet in its earliest conception out of primordial and cosmic matter, and when the Earth has served its purpose, I say verily it disintegrateth in thought. It returns to the elements from whence it came. And man moves on and on into greater lessons of spirit as he comes ever more to know himself.

Man looks to his many sorrows and does not understand for through love alone has the heart of a Caesar been touched and has the trade stamp of truth been impressed upon his heart. Down through the ages love has wrought its own miracles, and the hungry heart of mankind is now more open than ever before. The hungry hearts of the world are crying now for truth, for they have starved on everything else. They have been given strict discipline, indulgent religions, and materialistic science, but the human heart has not responded to these disciplines, these cults, and these authoritative priests. And in that they have learned their great lesson, for now they know that only the emanations of Deity will satisfy their hunger, and they seek once again the sacred manna from heaven. We say verily the manna comes and it shall be seen of all men.

High in open heavens the host rushes unto you now. It is truly written of them: they do not slumber nor sleep. The latchet of their shoes is not broken; their chariots swift as the whirlwinds; their swords sharp for the harvest; and the people roar against them like the roaring of many lions. Behold, there is darkness and sorrow upon the land, beloved ones.

So often one mortal becomes engrossed with the things of the day until all of his energies are taken up and sapped of their strength by the futility of each day and its many blind alleys. Yet let us grasp at least a few moments of each day; Let us see the vision, --vision that shall soon leave the kingdom of visions and fantasias and the kingdom of illusion, and shall come down and dwell among us; and it shall be real and we can feel of its great substance. For have we not served a countless millennia in many lands, under many names, under many races? We have tasted of the fruits of many peoples of all flesh. Would that we could recount every single lifetime!--if we could but recount and recall each and every hand that has been laid upon our fevered brow in love, each stalwart arm of a young man that has supported us in our miseries and in our sorrows, the kind word of the loving neighbor or wife!

Let us remember the love that we have known through countless lives. These things are indelible. They exist forever in time; the kind pat on the back. All of these things are still existing in time somewhere some place, for love perpetuates itself and never dies. Only hate expends itself in fury as the uncontrolled vortex.

Dear ones, at this time we are going to send you now the ray and frequency of our beloved Master Teacher. Please forget your surroundings. Lose yourself. Let your mind float in emptiness as though you are in the hand of the Creator. I say that the Christ has never been more close to His followers, to His mentors, His servants, those beneath and below. Can you with limited mortality, can you try to place the picture from the beginning when you came to Earth until now? Can you try to glimpse it as one great picture? as one great service? Listen quietly now for the still small voice.

(Archangel Uriel Speaking)

(Archangel Michael Speaking)

It is my privilege to bring you these words of His. Beloved of my heart, listen for my voice in the sweetness of sleep, and listen for my voice as it wings its way toward you as the white dove of redemption. Listen! Watch, and wait! For the kingdom of which we spoke long time past now cometh upon the Earth scene. Verily men have said, since we preached and ministered, the kingdom is at hand. Beloved, the kingdom is here and now today. Let us make ourselves a living part of its being. So be it! So be it!

Archangel Michael Speaking
(Received 11/5/55)

Ave sheoi! If you could but know the glory, the glory that exceedeth creative light! If you could but know how the heavens rejoice this night! For as the Golden Helmeted Ones sweep around the Earth and around again, we know that this is the time when man, looking up into starlit night climbing the great rugged mountain, that there shall,--there shall come a day of great knowing to each heart.

Beloved, the day of the great telling that has been prophesied is now imminent in your affairs. You must now array yourself in full armor, as you have been tutored throughout all time. Do not fear the brilliance of the armor for it is your passport to higher realms. It is your shibboleth; it is your shield of the ages. Only by its effulgence shall you be known of man.

Spend more time in listening to the words of your Divine Father: one who shall speak in the plural and say, "These are my beloved sons in whom I am well pleased." The Four and Twenty Elders sit about the Throne waiting to receive you. You are now coming to a time when it is of vast importance that you speak out so that many souls might be lifted in their final stage of development. . Shortly all secrets shall be revealed in the light of the new day when nothing can stand that is hidden, nothing that is dark that shall not be exposed to the light. Some shall wither and decay; others shall spring forth in response to the new energy. All will be shown in its true form and state...

I cannot speak long for my light diminishes. My ray extended to you now retreats back to Source...But we speak not in riddles, nor do we speak in the beauteous language merely to make a pretty speech. There is meaning there. Mark this well. Mark it well! Let all thy services be toward it alone. Man now has attained the summit of his creation and perfection on Earth. It has served its age-long purpose, and now he stands atop a mountain. Man on Earth is enthroned as a god and does not even realize his own godhood!

Listen for the legions that march onward and ever onward, not those of the Black Dragon, not those of the black hordes of all space. Listen for the legions of the Light that penetrate your knowings. There shall be a great blinding light and crash of thunder. Then man shall stand naked before his Creator and man will <u>know</u>, for all history has only been lived and written that man may know! Man has scaled the heights and depths of his experience on Earth to attain the godhood of knowing. And out of the rumblings and dust of the past he will hear his own voice.

(Archangel Michael Speaking)

(Archangel Raphael Speaking)

<u>Some day soon, after the day of the great telling, a great multitude shall witness and hear the voice that speaks to them, the voice that swells as a thousand angel voices, yet one, that says, "Come home, Earth! Come home, Earth Come home!"</u> Michael of the Sun.

Archangel Raphael Speaking
(Received 11/5/55)

Rama Eloi, Rama Eloi, Eloi Rama, Eloi Rama.. This is Raphael of the Sun speaking...

Remember, as the new vibrations come in as a great tidal wave of spiritual truth, --and when I say "tidal wave" I mean the term literally and figuratively,-- but it will manifest on all planes: physical, mental, and spiritual. Remember that the great winds of the Creator embrace you; the grass longs to play with your feet, the winds with your hair. By this I mean you shall stand unashamed as the flame before the altar--the altar that is He who is our life.

The Golden Book is now open, the seal broken, never to be replaced; and in that Golden Book only a few names are written. Others who once lived on the world of Khar to later live on the world of Lucifer, now the Earth, they shall return to the vibration of Khar to work out their destiny. The Earth is the Dark Red Star of Creation.

You have no idea what shall be seen in the skies!--great spiritual manifestations! The entire world shall be on its knees! And the rock shall fall on those who seek a refuge--those who have sought their brother's life--to the ever watching army of the golden horde, the host of the golden chariots and the golden wing. I add the double-edged sword, which is the Sword of Truth that emanates from the Father's mouth. It shall not fail in its judgment!.... Raphael returning to the Source.

Archangel Michael Speaking
(Received 11/5/55)

Elohim, Elohim, Elohim! From all space, from all space, from all space, from all space, from all space! Elohim, Elohim, Elohim!

From this sphere of life now is emanating a golden mist that shall enclose your world even as from this sphere for countless millions of years your world has been enclosed in the golden radiance that has brought it heat and light, which is symbolic of the Father's Divine Love and Divine Wisdom--heat and light to warn man's physical being and to give him the flame of spiritual life. For it is the affinity between this sphere and yours that makes for life and makes it possible for you to search for Truth.

Now from this sphere are gathering the Golden Helmeted Ones who are now progressing toward your world: from all space, from all space the covenant of our Infinite Father, the covenant of the bow in the sky.

Shortly there shall be a bow that has never been seen before in the sky or Earth, a bow of magnificent color, from which emanates great musical sounds that shall come to the ear of all men, and they shall know a calling; they shall know a love; they shall know a duty. From this bow of beauty, this bow of duty that calls to its own, it shall first appear as a great violet radiance over the entire world: the Golden Helmeted Ones from our sphere who have never come so close to Earth before. Only in ages past have they appeared to Earth in a very few cases on very special errands for the INFINITE FATHER. And they were given the title of Archangels, the spiritual messengers who were above the angels or the messengers, the mentors of the messengers.

Now they do come for this final,--this final gathering of the chariots of gold when the chariots shall gather to subdue the last remains of the darkness of Earth; for over the entire world a great golden glow shall manifest itself, and, when it lifts, those who remain will know truly they are their brother's keeper. This is our part of the mission. This is our part that we serve, for it will not be long when this sphere itself is no longer of use. And this is always the job of those who live in the very center of their solar system, those who live under the great golden corona of light. Man has always looked to this great orb for his very life, and rightly so that he should.

Oh, man of Earth! that you would awaken! awaken to these new chords that are not lost chords. Indeed they have never been lost! Always they have remained--the five stringed lute that man of Earth would play and yet not understand the music thereof.

Now there is a new chord, a note that is real--not weird--but full of zeal for the men of Earth who would themselves apply feathers and wax to develop wings that they might fly up to the great Sun Body, for in this legend of the youth who would fly to the Sun--and yet his wings were melted--there lies a truth that man wished to fly to this great body which gave him life, for he believed that by being encompassed within it he would find himself and find the eternal mystery of mysteries. For the ancient peoples of your world did not believe that this body was one of great flames and heat; they understood its true meaning as the center and life of this System.

Now this body is in great age, as celestial bodies do age. It has existed for fifteen hundred billion years. Now it shall die. It shall, because of the increased vibrations, explode, announcing its end to the far corners of the Universe as a great exploding star. But the end is a beginning, for it has served us well and we march on! Humanity of this System marches on, my beloved children, to other portions of the Father's realm.

Yet this orb shall not end until the Millennium has passed, when once again the forces of darkness are released. Then shall the end come and this System disintegrates in thought, for it is only thought, --since all celestial bodies, whether star or world, remember, beloved ones, these are only--they are only the forms in which our Father's words are formed. They are His words that were spoken in the beginning that there should be light and there should be substance. They are His words, and some shall disintegrate in thought--that which was only thought in the beginning.

Someday, dear ones, in the not too distant future, you shall look upon a great purple plain ahead, a golden light that draws you to it by its great heat and warmth. Imagine, dear ones, what awaits those of Earth who have proved themselves to be His children! They shall not want for truth. For many centuries our Father has heard the words of the sincere on Earth: "Our Father, thy will be done on Earth as it is in heaven." This prayer is now to be answered.

It shall be on Earth as it is in heaven. Man shall no longer want for anything. He shortly shall take his place as true son of God, for did not your Master, Jesus the Christ, say: "Know ye not that ye are gods?" Know this and accept the scepter and orb of your godhood, not that you would exalt yourselves above your fellow-men, but that you accept the gift that the Father has always kept waiting for His children who would but see the light.

And you shall step foot on plains or unbelievable grandeur--you and the others of Earth who are the harvest which the angels now come to reap. This harvest shall be gathered tenderly and bound together and stacked in the fields awaiting the proper light that has an affinity with their light. And then they shall vanish from the

136

Earth. In a twinkling they shall be gone. Then they shall come into a great natural amphitheater and, while all the angels, as it is written in your Holy Scriptures,--the Holy Scriptures that were written on command and authority of the Light from this sphere--these Scriptures that say: the heavenly host shall sing before His throne. It is true. It is truly written this shall be.

And when the singing takes place it is singing that has never been heard on Earth, for it is a mingling of the souls of all those who partake of this fellowship. Great animals and birds partake in this vibrational singing of the spheres. And you shall see before your eyes a fantasia of beauty and color and sound and harmony mingling together in worship to the Light that is the I AM. Amamaru...

And then you shall see opening up before you great beautiful flowers and trees and vines, and they sway to and fro in response to your singing, and open their lovely petals and faces, straining upward, turning to look at the Sun. All the Father's Creation--not only man--but all that has been placed here shall respond together for, as we see you from this sphere, you are not countries or nations or individuals or animals or slaves or free, you are one being, the being that is Earth. You are one MAN, a man with many wounds, who shall soon be free and soothed by his wounds.

And now a great wing as of a great angelic messenger and herald sweeps the Earth and this wing gathers its own into its fold. Like a comb it covers the Earth and sweeps gently down the wing of a golden mist.

Beloved ones, join in fellowship this evening for this day, according to your science of numerology, is the day of nine, a universal number, the number of the Master Jesus. This is a nine. It is not coincidence that you have met this night.

May I say that it is a great honor to me to be able to enter into your fellowship and into your place of work, into your hearts. Dear ones, even though you go about your mundane activities of the day, search the deepest part of your heart. Realize with joy this is the time we have been waiting for! Let your fellow-man know the Master soon shall place His foot upon Earth again. This is the time when all men can rejoice! The bells of heaven are sounding! The trumpets are sounding!

Those of the Golden Helmets march on! They are streaming forth from this sphere to the Earth! Aram-maru! Aramu-maru! Blessings and love and light as our hearts touch your hearts. This is Michael of the Sun. Aramu...

Archangel Gabriel Speaking
(Received 11/5/55)

Ave...! Gabriel of the Star Craft speaking...

They do not mean what is written; they do not mean: "Father, Father, why hast thou forsaken me?" Why would the Master, who vowed constantly the Aton--the ONE GOD--why would He in desperation finally doubt the Father and say, "Why hast thou forsaken me?" These are words of cowards! These are the words of those who have not fulfilled their mission, not the words of the Christ! These have been misinterpreted, for they are not in the Aramaic language of the time. They are in the most ancient Solar or Mother Tongue which, of course, the Master would revert to at that

138

time. The words are not "sabachthani"; they are spelled with a "z"--
"zbacthani": z-b-a-c-t-h-a-n-i. "Eli, Eli, lama zbacthani" means:
"Those who defame me shall keep open my wounds"--"those who
defame me shall keep open my wounds": "Eli, Eli, lama zbacthani."
"Father, unto thee I commend my spirit; it is finished."

Now the music you play sets the theme. What is it as the great
war machines of the world are now messing together? In the Holy
Land we see the beginning of the end for Earth. Once again Egypt
and Israel--is it not significant, my dear ones? --Egypt and Israel.
And it shall grow and grow. The greatest battle that has ever been
seen shall take place, not only amongst those who fight their fellow-
man but the elements, the Earth itself, shall find a battlefield. The
forces of Nature shall be unleashed because of Man's wrong thinking
and doing: as he has worshiped in word and not deed, nor has he
served the Master.

What a great time it was when the heralds of heaven peeled forth
the announcement that this night "Peace on Earth" for He--He who
was Buddha, He who was the light of Asia, the "Light of the World"
that manifested in the humble surroundings that night!

I was Gabriel of the Sun, as my Brothers, but since that time I
have been Gabriel of the Star Craft until this work is completed.

The armies shall be stopped by a great natural cataclysm. The
weapons shall melt in their hands. They will find finally that the
Earth has reached the place where no longer will the vibrations
tolerate an act of wanton murder on the part of its inhabitants. For
centuries man has spilled blood upon the Earth over and over again!

No one moment of one day has passed without a man's blood being spilled upon the Earth. Now the vibration refused to kill.

It will not be an act of the Father; it will not be an act of superior military equipment; it will be man's own thinking rebounding upon him. By his thinking over many, many thousands of years the vibration has been created. Finally, in the great war when man raises his weapons against his fellow-man, they will not function in the new vibration, Anything that will cause destruction will melt. If a man utters a destructive word, he will disintegrate. Anything negative will vanish.

All government and authority must collapse, as it is written, before He returns. We do not preach sedition; we do not preach tyranny or the acts of traitors; we preach Jesus Christ!

How can this nation of the United States of America or any nation on the Earth claim that it is following the Master as it builds greater forces of destruction, greater ways of killing fellow-man! Your leaders say--they say that it is true--it is a great truth that the more power they have the more peace we shall have. You do not have peace by placing a gun in a man's back! What kind of a peace is this? It is the peace of idiots and fools. It is the peace of those who serve Amun, who serve Satan!

When the Master was Buddha He uttered the great truth: "How and when will hate cease if it is met with more hate?"

Your country is not Christian! It is not following the Master Jesus! If it was it would lay down all arms; it would destroy all of its atomic weapons; it would have no weapons of destruction or

140

protection. It would rely on Him _alone_ to protect them. _He_ is the only protection. Therefore, this country which was prepared to lead the world now must go down with that world, as it was written.

All nations, and I do repeat, all shall collapse utterly and completely with every organization that exists upon the face of your Earth! And then the new government with Christ as King, as it is written, and the house of David once again reigns supreme!

And now from out of the land that is the oldest comes murmurings and undercurrents. The handwriting is on the wall between Egypt and Israel this night. Again the great Star shall shine on that border. The world shall become the footstool, as it is written.

Yes, there shall be those things, those portents and signs, the like of which the world has never seen before! The seas shall rage! The monsters of another age shall roam the land! The great creatures that once lived, weighing many, many tons, shall again roam the streets! Famine shall appear!--great pestilence of locusts! The seas shall give up monsters that the Earth thought long dead! and they shall crawl on the shores!

And all these things soon; but have we not prepared? Are we not made for this time? knowing that out of it shall come the greatest good of all for all men everywhere as they progress in ever expanding grandeur up, and up, and up, and up, until they reach the heart of God. And when they reach the heart of God, there shall be other hearts to ascend to on and on ad infinitum. Truly it is said, "Quo vadis Domino?"--Whither goest thou, Lord?" We shall always say, "Whither goest thou, Lord?" as He receives every promise in His progression. And when we become lords and gods and rulers of universes even, He shall still be the Lord and we shall be called yet His friends.

I speak now of world government, with your permission. Atlantis shall again have a Poseid. Lemuria shall again have a Zorai. The Inca shall have their Inca. And Egypt shall have a Pharaoh. In Egypt, one of the great centers of world government, as a new Pharaoh starts a new dynasty, it shall be known in millennia to come by historians as "The Golden Dynasty." The great seven colonies of the Motherland are returning, as well as the Motherland. The Brotherhood at Lake Titicaca will return the great Golden Sun Disc to the Temple of the Sun.

And you do not know, but this day you have a great voice in the world. Why is she appearing in the public places of the Earth? Why is she singing the ancient songs of her people the Incas? It is not an accident. Every great major city of the world she appears in she is establishing a vibration for a purpose.

Yes, the new government of the world shall be based on the ancient government of the Sun, which modern scientists do not understand. It was not the worship of the Sun itself! It was the purest form: the adoration of Aton--the at-one-ment that the Master created by the giving of His blood that poured from His side on Golgotha. It established the vibration in the Earth that made forever,--forever the eternal ray from the Earth to the Father, a ray that will not end. This was the purpose and meaning of His death on Calvary.

Would the Great CREATOR of ALL send HIS Son to die in despair and failure on the cruel Cross? His implies that the CREATOR admitted defeat. HE makes no errors! We make error!

HE never makes error! Jesus came to the Earth to <u>LIVE</u>, not to <u>die</u>! Tell that to your churches! They say, "Jesus came to die so that all men might be saved by the shedding of His blood." This is sacrilege! He did not come to die. If He came to die why would the Father have sent Him in the first place? They imply in their very fundamental and narrow teachings that Jesus came to teach men, but they rejected the truth, and therefore God, His Father, had no alternative but to place His Son on the cruel Cross so that through the shedding of His precious blood all men might be saved and secure for themselves an everlasting and eternal free passage and quick ticket to paradise. This is the mouthing of Amun! It is not the teachings of our heavenly Father.

Tell them Jesus did not come to die! Take Jesus off the Cross! Do not place Him on the walls of your churches on the Cross. He is not on the Cross! He is not the dead Christ! Their entire gospel is based on the fact that Jesus died for them. He <u>LIVED</u> for them, dear ones; He did not <u>die</u> for them! We must follow his teachings, His words, His life. Instead they are living in the shadow of His death! They do not <u>live</u> His teachings, and they call themselves Christian nations! They are not Christian. They follow the Dark One!

Their munitions factories, their secret smoke-filled chambers are not the chambers where the Christ would come. That is why this farce, this United Nations, shall collapse. On the surface it is the sheep's clothing, but inside it is a ravening beast! It is not based truly on the life of the Master. If they would forget about His death and how it secured them an easy way into heaven, they could solve the world situation. This you have realized and you know as a truth, do you not?

But they have been given their chance. It is too late now. The sickle is being thrust into the field. The fire is being set to the altar that shall determine what is chaff, what is pure gem. The stubble shall be burned; only the gems shall remain.

A great government shall arise in Egypt in the New Millennium--a new Pharaoh for Egypt. Those who were the Twelve shall sit in high places. Those of the Seventy shall instruct the peoples. Remember, a new Inca shall rule that country. Their praises, as they lead their people, will set the vibration for the Millennium.

Dear Ones, for the next several decades the Earth shall be wrapped in chaos of the very worst kind. The Earth shall switch her axes, not once but three times! Dante with his inferno could not picture such tragedy! I am not a prophet of gloom; I am a prophet of the facts. Because it is tragic, yes, but it is more tragic to see this continue. The quicker it is eliminated the quicker the great vibrations are established, the better for all men. Even those who perish shall be released to go on and learn where they must learn.

The law is no retrogression--only progression. There are only a few people on Earth at this time who can progress in this environment. All others shall vanish in one way or another.

At this moment a great comet heads for the Earth, great comet that is bigger than the Earth, eleven times bigger than the Earth. It comes from the region of Vega. It is foretold in the Book of John that a great stone shall hit the Earth as the Earth passes through the tail of this comet.

The government of the Earth, the very heart and headquarters of it, shall not be on the Earth. There will be twelve who will sit as representatives in the council of Earth who rule as Pharech, Inca, Zorai, and Poseid, and the others. But He who rules the Earth as His footstool shall not then be on the Earth. And I would speak not in riddles, although Gabriel is known to speak in riddles. It is only a riddle to those of little understanding. But the real government of the Earth shall be from another Star, yet not a Star of millions of miles of distance, a Star that becomes the Earth and is attached to the Earth, a Star that shall be known as "Zebeka Musor," a School of Life.

Let it be known this night that Gabriel has passed this way again... Ave....! I hear violet calling me back. I return through the Seven th Ray, the great ray, to The Star once again... Gabriel returns, "Eli, Eli, lama zbacthani." "Eli, Eli, laza zbacthani,"--"Eli, lama zbacthani"!

Archangel Michael Speaking
(Received 2/4/56)

Ave sheoi: Ave! Ave sheoi! I follow the line of the great Golden Helmeted ones who are continuously circling the Earth Planet, more and more increasing in numbers and in strength.

For a moment, if you will, go back with me to a very remote age of antiquity far greater than I could comprehend in terms of Earth years, and picture in your mind, if you will, a great spiraling mass of violet blue flame spiraling upward, ever upward, leading man on to ever expanding grandeur in the Universe of our Father.

Before Sananda, before the Father, it was Loslo. Remember what Sananda has said: "I know of no other great Spirit beyond the Father. He is the Ancient of Days. I know, beloved ones, of no other beyond Him, yet I know that there are others beyond Him. I believe they exist."

What is this hierarchy of Gods, of Creators, in the Omniverse? And I do wish to emphasize this so that you may understand the terminology. It is true, as some of you have suggested, God the Father is the Father that Sananda. speaks of. He is a Creator-God, a Creator-God of ancient mythology and legend. He is the God--God the Father--thought incarnate on the Star Sun Sirius. But there are Gods beyond Him of magnificence beyond comprehension.

There are worlds in space where man is nothing but ever changing color and hue, worlds of fantastic iridescence and glowing beauty, where one form mingles with the other, always one, always changing. There are worlds where man becomes only a beautiful tone as a tinkling bell, where life is only a kaleidoscope of fantastic nature, worlds that we cannot even begin to comprehend, that would make God the Father-thought incarnate on Sirius--appear as a grain of sand on a lonely beach.

Yet above all of this the Omniverse itself is the ALL, THE PERFECT ONE, the INFINITE FATHER, the ALL CREATOR, the SELF CREATED ONE, and we call HIM in our Order simply EVERNESS. Sheita maieta!...

The world has called the Star Sun, the Blue-White Star of the Father, S-i-r-i-u-s-. I might add, that is where the word "serious" developed: s-e-r-i-o-u-s...

146

Dear ones, what is behind this great plan now unfolding upon the Earth? There is a greater plan beyond, even beyond the migration from this Solar System, as we gave you before, and the answer to that is that we are being called from out of the depths, depths of night in space to serve those who cry out to us.

Do you know what the schoolroom of Earth is really for? Do you know why all the tears and sorrow and death and misery and anguish, on Earth has been for? For personal development, yes, but what else? What is the grander, greater plan? Only that a world will become a cinder through an atomic war? No! What is the classroom of Earth? Is it geometry, English, history, or Spanish? What is the lesson to be learned?--so that Spirit may come to know itself, so that man will be freed from the blight of the great adultery!

Now comes the time as those of the Golden Helmets swing out from the great Solar Body! This is the time of the GREAT TRANSMUTATION! Ishtal Maxin.

One day on your Earth shall come a blinding flash of light. All the old shall pass away, burned as chaff on the altar of truth! Only the gems will remain, the gems that can withstand the Eternal Flame.

It would be hard for most to understand or to even believe what the Earth is for, for it appears to be exactly the opposite of its true mission. The Earth, dear ones, is a school for gods. Man--the small harvest of man upon the Earth--man who has lost the vestiges of the human, -- there are those on Earth today. Remember it is written, not that the harvest is great; or is it? Yes, it is written thus: and the laborers few. The harvest is great according to the laborers, but from the total of the Earth's population, the harvest is small. The Earth is now nearly two and three-quarter billions of people. Only one to ten out of every thousand will remain, and only one-tenth of one percent of these shall fulfill their missions.

And it has taken millions of years since man has been upon the Earth to bring about this one small concentrated small drop of life to evolve in the crucible of time. Yet that small group, the Earth with all its negative force, its constant buffeting, --remember nothing is as strong as the rock upon which the winds of time blow, upon which the sands, the eternal sands, blow ceaselessly and erode away, --but the great rock stands.

Yes, the Earth is a classroom for godhood, --not Mars, not Venus, not Jupiter, not glorious magnificent Saturn, not spiritual. Neptune, Pluto, or Mercury--not even the Sun and its many bodies and its greet life--the Earth! because any entity or soul that rises up from the Earth is as you have been told and as it is written in the sacred books.

Remember, the great lotus rises from the slime of earth. And now there is a single bloom. And the Father looks down from blue of sky and gold of Sun and the Father sees a single pure lotus opening from the slime, and shortly He reaches down and plucks it and removes it to take it home again.

Therefore you and your fellow-men everywhere are being conditioned for the GREAT TRANSMUTATION. And then--and, as those of the Golden Helmets, we march on to other universes and worlds that call and need our help. When man achieves his graduation day, when he achieves his godhood, then the work begins. Over countless millions of years man has risen from animal to become angel again! Think of the lives and the intrigues, the battles, and the loves that have gone on to produce one drop of the eternal elixir!

Let us lose ourselves in this ever expanding army, a living thing that shall one great dawn on your world shine forth as a golden glow over all the Earth. Those that run to the rocks will not find shelter. No bomb-proof shelter will give adequate safety. No mountain top, no cavern is deep enough, and no mountain top high enough, for this is the day of the GREAT TRANSMUTATION when all elements shall be changed. Not only are you being prepared for other atmospheres, but you are now changing dimensions. You are leaving the world, the kingdom of the third dimension. You are entering the dimension of understanding. Accept that which the Father has for you.

Realize that the physical as it is developed is only to serve for a brief time your fellow-man. Work as one for, even though you know it not, you stand at this very moment before the Throne of God the Father.

Some day we shall together look back upon our Solar System with all its great development and we shall see it explode like a great exploding star in the farthest corner of the Father's realm, because then when it has served its purpose it disintegrates in thought. So be it! Selah! Selah!

We are an army, in truth an army,. There are corners of the Omniverse yet where there is no light--only darkness,--and even a great army can only appear as a small pinpoint of candlelight as the candle that shines this night. But remember, dear ones, the great

149

truth that no matter how vast the darkness, no matter how vast the night, one small candle flame holds back that great darkness. In its insignificance it is absolutely invincible because it is light.

And then as a tiny candle flame we shall burst forth into an area that has never known light before and the, as they have said, "It is beautiful," we bring, even as the workers brought to ancient Egypt, the light, through Akhnaton. The people had never seen it before. Some it blinded them. It was too bright. They did not understand any more than they understand today because of its great blinding light. It was a thing to be shunned, to be afraid of, to be rejected, and many fell back into the comfort of darkness.

Man is afraid of dark? We say, no; this is not true! Man is afraid of light! He wishes once again to be in the darkness of the womb where there is no light, for there alone he feels safety, warmth, and life. It takes courage to go into the light--not the dark.

Yes, oh, living Aton! bear us up on thy eternal wings unto our destiny! Ishtal Maxin. Michael of the Sun.

Archangel Gabriel Speaking
(Received 2/4/56)

Ave...! Ave...! Ave...! Gabriel.

… There have been confusions as they beat upon the mind with fury for the Earth Planet. Although those of Earth call Mars the god of war, Saturn the god of gloom, Neptune the god of mystery, Pluto the god of Hades, no!-- those are the attributes of the Red Star, the Earth; gloom, despair, death, war! This planet has been in the grasp

150

and is in the grasp of the great black hordes from a great distant galaxy, known to those of the Oriental world as the hideous order of the Black Dragons, the great black horde, now incarnate on the Earth in Communism and all totalitarian movements. They sit on all the thrones of Earth. Verily I say, they sit on all the thrones of Earth, whether it is "E Pluribus Unum," the "Hammer and Sickle," or "Justice, Equality, and Fraternity."

This.... knew that night above Bethlehem. She knew that there were the workers already upon Earth who were performing the task that they had come for-- the Lesser Avatars who came to do this work, who had come not just at this time but who had come countless millennia before. They had served with this Teacher, whether he was Buddha, Zoroaster, Melchizedek, Shem, and others. But she knew that her duty would be fulfilled upon the Earth for the first incarnation upon that world and the last incarnation upon that Red Star when He would come again for the day, Michael's day of the GREAT TRANSMUTATION.

The black hordes are now suffering the death throes of the Dragon, and in the death throes of a beast many will perish, but remember this: the beast goes down to defeat. The martyrs of God shall rejoice!

Sananda said: "Look what they have done to the Master! If this is so, what will they do to the servants?" Your heart and your soul and your work and your hand must touch the brow of those who are constantly turning their eyes upward, looking for that great cloud that shall come. Your presence will still their souls, and then one day you shall walk by their sides rejoicing and singing, as it is truly written? "The fields and all the trees shall clap their hands with joy," for we go out in peace as we are taken up in the hand, as we gather where the eagles gather and find we are in His hand once again.

Ave...! Ave...! Ave...! Rest and develop thy strength, and receive thy strength from the Eternal Flame that is always available,--the Blue-White Flame that shall shortly burst into flame once again on the Red Star, turning its redness into the violet ray of completion.

If man upon Earth knew that each and every soul is precious in His sight, no matter how degraded, no matter how impure, no matter how rejected or not by man! All shall eventually rise at the sound of a great calling and move on as one. Man is destined to be placed upon the throne of the Omniverse to survey all stars, planets, suns, worlds, which are HIS thoughts in action. They all move to one responsive chord.

The ultimate?--there is no ultimate. There is only living, --but first serving. But one day we shall only be music that responds perfectly.

Love, peace, and harmony. So be it!

An Alert
(Received 9/12/56)

Master K. H. Speaking

Blessings, dear ones. K. H.

The first part of this message is directed to those who serve in the Light. Before long a purge may come to some of you who serve in the Light, but take no heed. And then I want you to use as a reference and a proof to them a certain Scripture from the Gospel of St. Mark, Chapter 13, Verses 9-20.

St. Mark 13:9-20: "But take heed to yourselves; for they shall deliver you up to councils; and in the synagogues ye shall be beaten: and ye shall be brought before rulers and kings for my sake, for a testimony against them. And the gospel must first be published among all nations. But when they shall lead you, and deliver you up, take no thought beforehand what ye shall speak, neither do ye premediate; but whatsoever shall be given you in that hour, that speak ye: for it is not ye that speak, but the Holy Ghost.

Now the brother shall betray the brother to death, and the father the son; and children shall rise up against their parents, and shall cause them to be put to death. And ye shall be hated of all men for my name's sake: but he that shall endure unto the end, the same shall be saved. But when ye shall see the abomination of desolation, spoken of by Daniel the prophet, standing where it ought not, (let him that readeth understand,) then let them that be in Judaea flee to the mountains: And let him that is on the housetop not go down into the house, neither enter therein, to take any thing out of his house: And let him that is in the field not turn back again for to take up his garment. But woe to them that are with child, and to them that give suck in those days! And pray ye that your flight be not in the winter. For in those days shall be affliction, such as was not from the beginning of the creation which God created unto this time, neither shall be. And except that the Lord had shortened those days, no flesh should be saved: but for the elect's sake, whom he hath chosen, he hath chosen, he hath shortened the days."

They say there is no chance of such a thing taking place. There is!--in the Holy Scripture. Also, they are the same ones who say ther'll be no wars; ther'll be no catastrophe: all is peace; all is love. But there is the message in Sananda's own words! is it not? as recorded by Mark. They are true words as Mark heard them himself. Because they will deliver you up. I tell you verily, dear ones, it is the Holy Ghost but it is the Father who will speak through you. You have nothing to fear from them. Tell that to these dear ones to whom you are sending out these messages. That is the message that K. H. would send to the sheep.

And now if you will, please turn to Revelation, Chapter 3, Verses 14-22. We're giving them Bible; we're giving them proof along with what we're saying because we know they like Bible, and some of them don't like it the way we're doing it because it's true. There's nothing "putrid" in the word of the Father or in the Master's words. The putrefaction is within themselves.

Rev. 3:14-16: "And unto the angel of the church of the Laodiceans write; These things saith the Amen, the faithful and true witness, the beginning of the creation of God; I know thy works, that thou art neither cold nor hot; I would thou wert cold or hot. So then because thou art lukewarm, and neither cold nor not, I will spue thee out of my mouth."

There! what more do they want! He is saying again: "This is the Master speaking." In the new Bible version it says, "I will vomit you up." He would rather have you completely indifferent to His word than lukewarm because you know the truth and yet you exercise it not. Were that you were cold, ignorant of the facts! "I would rather have you cold or hot but not lukewarm." Lukewarm Christians will

154

be spewed out of the mouth of the Elder Brother and the Father. Yes, indeed!

Tell them: where is your faith?--if you do not believe in the promises that He has given. If we are His children, yea even his sons, will He not be with us? Lukewarm Christians beware!

Rev. 3:17: "Because thou sayest, I am rich, and increased with goods, and have need of nothing; and knowest not that thou art wretched, and miserable, and poor, and blind, and naked..."

"Yes, I am a good Christian. I go to church every Sunday. I haven't missed a Sunday in twenty-five years. You see that panel in the church window over there--that new frosted glass panel--I donated that to the church; it cost $99.50. I give to the missionary funds, to the building funds, to the hospital funds, to the orphan fund. I am rich; I have plenty. I am a Christian, but I don't believe the promises of God. I don't even believe in eternal life. I doubt it at times; in fact; I doubt it quite often, I don't like to think of death because really I don't believe in eternal life. I worry about my illnesses and about my troubles, but I don't take them to the Father who has Promised He will do all and take care of all. I don't have the faith." Go on.

Rev. 3:18-22: "I counsel thee to buy of me gold tried in the fire, that thou mayest be rich; and white raiment, that thou mayest be clothed, and that the shame of thy nakedness do not appear; and anoint thine eyes with eyesalve, that thou mayest see. As many as I love, I rebuke and chasten: be zealous therefore, and repent, Behold, I stand at the door, and knock: if any man hear my voice, and open the door, I will come in to him, and will sup with him, and he with

155

me. To him that overcometh will I grant to sit with me in my throne, even as I also overcame, and am set down with my Father in his throne. He that hath an ear, let him hear what the Spirit saith unto the churches."

Yes, he that has an ear; tell your people that is the gist of my message tonight: he that hath an ear, let him listen. Lukewarm Buddhist, lukewarm Mohammedan (Moslem--or whatever he might be), lukewarm Christian: the Master stands at the door and knocks! It is high time that we forget our lukewarmness. Be either cold or be hot!--but be one or the other! But I would suggest that now you begin to burn with a <u>fervor</u>, the fervor that those blessed martyrs of old burned with.

This is the time, as we have told you, of revolution! It's a time for those of pure of heart to rise up and put down the dark forces of the Earth. This is not a time for "lollygagging" in churches on Sunday! This is not a time for lukewarmness, half heartedness! This is not a time… to be going around in secular societies, worried in church over the Ladies' Aid. Get on fire, Christians! because the very negative "Black" forces are deluding you! <u>Wake up</u>!!! Lukewarmness--you'll be vomited out of the Master's mouth. He won't even bother with you! Because if you're cold--He's rather have you cold! because if you're cold He can convert you; He can use you. If you're hot you can be His divine evangelist. If you're lukewarm you're of no use whatsoever.

So once again I'm on my fiery tour. And I do enjoy how people cannot accept this as Master K. H. because K. H. is supposed to be a silly monk sitting on the roadside on his spikes contemplating the Sun, as I said before. I'm supposed to be uttering utterances or writing some sort of a poem. They believe that periodically from out of Shigatse I should make some such utterance: "That within the thousand petaled lotus dwells all wisdom: God is love; God is peace. Blessings Earth children." Rubbish! This is a time for men and masters of action! not a time to meditate upon the thousand petaled lotus, of the Sun, or anything else!

This is the time of the end that Sananda spoke of. Sananda was a man of action! When Sananda stood before the tomb of Lazarus did He say, "Please, Lazarus, come out." He said, "COME FORTH! COMMAND! IN THE NAME OF THE FATHER!" Lukewarmness is not of the Father. Be strong! Know wherein ye speak and wherein ye stand.

If, and I say "if" at any time you are delivered up... in this life or a million lifetimes henceforward, think not what you will say. But if you must speak outside of the Father and you must speak of your own volition, say that you have a mission upon the Earth, that you have deceived no one, no country, no thing. You are only serving the true CREATOR. Tell them you are answerable to no one for your actions but your CREATOR. And they will say, "Carry him away and crucify him," even as they did the Master, "for speaking such blasphemy," that you are calling yourself a son of God. And yet the poor fools do not know that they too are sons of God.

I must go. My fiery tour has been short, but I wanted to give you that to show you about being delivered up, and I wanted to give you that which speaks of the lukewarmness of the Christians. Tell them not to find themselves a member of the Church of Laodicea. Come out of that state of consciousness. Arise from your lethargic state!--

the lethargy that's been placed upon you by the negative forces, the anti-Christ. Wake up! DO NOT BE DECEIVED!!!

Blessings and love from the Eternal Source to you all, from Shigatse.

Sananda

Blest of my being: Be ye prepared to receive that which has been kept for 'them' for this time, and so be it given unto them in the name of the father, son and holy ghost, amen and beleis.

Blest ones, which are my sheep, and which I call my own, and which the Father has given unto me. Shall ye not see me and shall ye not walk and talk with me? For I have called thee out from among then. And some of you have heard my voice, and they have made haste unto me, and some have not heard, and they shall be made to hear. For I shall give unto them that which shall cause them to hear. And I shall bring them out from among them.

And ye shall be sibored in the eternal verities. And ye shall be given comprehension. And ye shall be at peace, and ye shall not hunger, nor shall ye know sorrow. For it is given unto me to care for my own and I shall be unto thee all that ye shall have need of. And so be it and beleis.

I am come into the world of men at the appointed hour, and I have kept my covenant with thee: for I said I should return unto thee - so have I, and I have gone the long way to keep my word: for it is given unto me to keep my word, And as I have promised thee, "I have prepared a place for thee," and now it is the day of thy preparation.

And as ye have been told, it shall be given unto every man to stand before the throne and to receive his sonship. And for that have I come that ye may receive that which is kept for thee. So be it that ye shall be given a new part and ye shall be prepared to receive it in the name of the father, son and holy ghost, amen and beleis. Be ye as ones which know where in ye are staid: and be ye alert, and watchful, for there are many sent unto thee that they may bring thee out. And ye shall receive them in the name of the Father which has sent them unto thee. For it is the day of much activity, and ye shall not be deceived for we guard "our own" and give unto them comprehension to know them which are sent.

Yet, ye shall pray for comprehension, and ye shall be unto thy self true, and ye shall have no 'false gods' for ye shall seek thy salvation thru the Father, and ye shall not seek in dark places, for there in is not light. And ye shall be as one which can see the light of the Christ, and walk there in. And ye shall be as the child of light.

Ye shall not ask any mans opinion nor council with the dead, for it is not given unto them to deliver thee out of darkness: and forget not that they too seek their freedom. And so be ye as one which can keep thy own council, and be thy own carter, and ye shall find thy way into the place which I have prepared for thee. And so be ye prepared to receive me, for I shall reveal myself unto them which are so prepared to receive me. So be it and beleis. Blest are they which seek me out, for they shall receive that which I have kept for them.

And now the day of revelation is come ye shall stand in the secret place of my abode and ye shall see and hear, and ye shall know that which ye hear and see. And ye shall council with me and ye shall be made to comprehend that which I shall say unto thee. So be ye prepared and as ye are prepared to receive me ye shall be prepared to receive of the Father which has sent me. And as ye are prepared to receive me so shall ye receive them which I shall send unto thee as my emissaries - for they shall go out before me - even as my father has sent me out before him! And so be it that many shall be sent in the name of the father, son and holy ghost, amen and beleis.

I am thy elder brother and servant of the Christ, which ye shall come to know. So be it and beleis. Sananda, order of the emerald cross and brotherhood of the 7 Rays.

Michael

Blest of earth, and them which are my sheep: I am come unto thee that ye may have more food, and of greater strength. I am in the place where in the pasture is green, and where in the waters are sweet. I am prepared to receive thee, for the pasture wherein I am is 'new' and the fertile valleys and rolling hills beckon unto thee.

Within this place are many shepherds and they know their flock, and they have been prepared to move them to higher ground where in is an abundance of everything which ye shall need.

I am in the place where in I shall receive my own, and they shall not want, for it is given unto me to provide for my own and there in is the fathers will. And so be it that ye too shall do the will of the

160

father for he has kept thee for this day. And so shall it be that ye shall return unto him, and he shall receive thee in love and mercy.

Be ye prepared for that which shall be fortuned unto thee of the father for he has kept a portion for thee which shall be given unto thee within the time which is near. And be it such as shall profit thee, and so be it and selah.

I am thy shepherd and sibor and servant of the father in the light of the Christ which ye shall come to know, Michael. School of the 7 Rays. Recorded by sister thedra, School of the 7 Rays. Lake Titicaca, Peru-Bolivia.

What has happened?

A revelation concerning the rapture of the Christian Church

What I (Olav Rogde) have written here came to me by inward vision on the 11th of December, 1952 in the afternoon. At the time I was at prayer in a Christian brother's home in Bergen. I was very seized with the vision, and it came to me when my mind was not at all occupied with any thought of the return of Christ for His Church.

It came to me that I should write an account of the revelation, but it did not appear to me to be a true vision. Supposing it to be my imagination I wanted to put it away from me, but inwardly I could get no peace. I said to the Lord:

"I can't remember all this! Is it to be written down? You must give it to me again."

After a few weeks, it was repeated. It was as though I sat down and read a story from a newspaper or book. This occurred at 10 o'clock at night. I found a pencil and an old cash-book, in which I began to write. I wrote and wrote, almost to one o'clock in the morning until I could not continue any longer. (I was 79 years old.) I asked the Lord for some rest and asked that if He desired to reveal any more that it might be given to me the next day. I then went to bed and fell asleep.

After a week the vision returned again at 10 o'clock at night. It was a direct continuation from the point at which I had previously stopped.

My hope and prayer are that my little publication will be used to revive some soul. --Olav Rogde.

The Vision

It was 3 o'clock in the afternoon, and Mrs. Andersson was sitting by the wireless listening to the children's program. It was very good today, she thought, with a little religion included. She considered a little religion good for the children, although it must not be too much, for that could become unbalanced...

Suddenly, after it had continued for a few minutes, the broadcast was interrupted. There was a sensational communique from Oslo to the effect that the whole city was in wild panic! The report was given as follows:

"Information received from the police states that something very strange has occurred. A large number, although it cannot yet be stated how many, of children and adults have vanished into space. The authorities cannot organize close search for them because too many people are involved. They ask that the families who have lost some relative or relatives will leave as detailed information as possible with the police, concerning where and how the disappearance happened. This is necessary in order that a correct survey of the position may be obtained and a solution to the mystery discovered."

Again, some minutes later a further announcement was made, stating that from a market place several shopkeepers had disappeared. An eye witness account was given, running thus:

"A woman tells us that she was about to pay for some flowers. The florist stood fumbling for change in a big bag when suddenly he completely disappeared. She heard him cry out: "Thank you, Jesus!" but she did not see him again. She rubbed her eyes, thinking there was a mist in front of her, but both man and the supposed mist had gone. At this moment a young woman nearby began to cry, staring at an empty perambulator. She began to run, shouting:

"Someone has stolen my child! Where is he? Where are the police?" Subsequently it was discovered that her child was an 8-months-old boy, and although the police were present there was found that nothing could be done.

Now shouts and cries were heard from everywhere. A big shopkeeper ran out of his shop crying:

'Help me! Help me!' Two of his assistants had simply vanished from their positions at the counter.

163

The position was worsening. Reports were now coming in from Stockholm stating that disappearances similar to these in Oslo had taken places and that all the city was in a panic. The radio announcements continued:

"It is known that several policemen are among the vanished people, and now Copenhagen and Helsinki have informed us of similar occurrences. From the countryside also reports are beginning to pour in, all concerning children and adults who have suddenly been taken away. In the face of this mystery police find themselves irresolute and powerless."

"Oh help us!" cried Mrs. Andersson, "Good God, what is it?" She moved away from the radio and went out of the house down to the gate, looking along the street with its fine little houses and trim gardens. Mrs. Haland was rushing toward her, fists to her eyes, shouting in agonized tones, "Ruth! Ruth! "

Catching sight of Mrs. Andersson, she asked: "Have you seen any stranger go by? Ruth has disappeared! She was sitting on the steps of our house, while I stood tending a rose bush, and suddenly she vanished! Absolutely! I shouted and cried, "Ruth!" but nobody answered me. I felt sure that something went along the road, but you know one gets so confused with a shock that one's mind plays tricks. One sees and thinks such strange things. But Ruth! Ruth! Where are you? Who has taken her?" She cried in desperation.

Suddenly Mrs. Andersson saw her husband coming. "What are you doing, coming home at this time?" she asked, "It's only half-past three."

"I can't do any more at work," he replied, "There is sheer confusion in the workshop. Many mechanics have disappeared in a mysterious way, several machines have stopped, and at first they thought an accident had caused the trouble. We searched around but didn't find a trace of any of the vanished people. I don't remember who it was, but one of the men who had said he was a Christian and had gone to meetings began to say: "Now it has happened! Now it has happened!" "What has happened?" I asked. "Jesus has fetched his people," he told me. He wrung his hands and cried and shouted: "Ad I am left!"

Mr. Andersson continued: "I asked him to be quiet, but he behaved worse and worse. It was awful to listen to him. There were probably several who were in the same state. In any case, we shall have to work outside normal hours for the time being."

Down in town the position was still worse. The traffic was completely congested. Drivers had vanished from their buses and cars, so had many passengers too. The trams had stopped and were standing in long lines, and the buses and cars which had drivers were still trying to move forward. People were half-crazed with fear and anxiety as they ran around looking for relatives. The police were powerless against such a tide of disaster.

Mrs. Haland was crying and wringing her hands as she ran back to her house. The radio was still on, and again one of the dreadful announcements, came over the air:

"There is now a news report from Bergen which speaks of vanished people everywhere. The telephones have been ringing constantly with inquiries and communications about this horrible event. From many ships people have vanished. All the new-born babies have vanished from the Maternity Hospitals, and the mothers are wailing in desperation. Assistants and nurses are panic-stricken, but even many of those have disappeared. "

At 11 o'clock the radio broadcast a communique from London which stated:

"Today at 3 o'clock, communications began to come in from all over the British Isles, stating that many adults and children have disappeared without leaving the slightest trace of their whereabouts. None of the vanished people have been found since, and this event is a complete mystery.

Some clergymen have called their parishioners together, and it has been found that the most God-fearing and praying people among their members are the ones who have been taken from their midst. Many clergymen and priests are also among the vanished people. As a result of these events, a bishop in a large religious community has called clergymen under his authority to attend a meeting tonight."

By this time there had elapsed 3 $^1/_2$ hours since the first report from Oslo, and events were proving that all the time new reports were arriving from countries all over the world with similar news concerning vanished people. From Korea in the Far East came the most sensational statement:

"In Korea, the number of vanished people is estimated at several hundred thousand, among them many military men from the United Forces."

To describe occurrences as they increased during those first hours would be quite impossible. In the streets people were running to and fro wringing their hands, especially the mothers who had lost their children. A large number of people, however, were deriding and cursing both God and people. One man came running down the street wringing his hands and shouting: "Take care! Take care! We will soon all be taken!" Probably he had lost his reason.

An elderly woman stood in a corner with folded hands, looking up at the sky. She was saying: "Oh no, not when we were not prepared and ready to go with Him when He came. Probably no one will be taken from now on. Good Lord, Jesus, help us! Now it has happened! I have been religious all my life but I never believed it would happen in this way and that He was to come in actual fact. I never believed everything so literally."

From the railway it was announced that in spite of everything no accidents had occurred. Only one train was standing at Finse without its driver and guard. An order was sent to all station-staffs to search carefully along the whole track for people who could possibly have jumped off the eastbound train, meeting with an accident as a result. This was because several travelers had disappeared. From the fjords and coastal shipping also more reports were sent, again concerning people disappearing from their posts.

Next appeared a paragraph in the newspapers, exhorting the people to be considerate and calm. It stated that the police and authorities were working everywhere to obtain an accurate estimate of the total number of vanished people. Scientists, especially meteorologists, were also at work - trying desperately to find the cause of this remarkable phenomenon.

Subsequently a report from the U.S.A. arrived, stating that information was coming in from the police in Eastern Europe similar to the news already received in Norway. Details were also forthcoming about terrible traffic troubles in U.S.A., together with many traffic accidents. The newspapers stated that the next day they would be receiving more detailed reports concerning events in the U.S.A.

At 8 o'clock that evening a news broadcast informed the public that the catastrophe was apparent in the same form throughout the whole world. Up to this time most was known about large towns and cities, but reports were subsequently being sent in from all parts of the countryside. The radio report continued:

"Many people have completely vanished. In the southern part of the world similar things have happened and appear to be exactly parallel with what we have seen here in Norway. "

A horrible anxiety was by now ruling everywhere. It seemed as though people dared not go to bed on this terrible night. In the streets hysterical discussions took place and more and more the opinion was growing that the mystery had to do with Christians and Christianity. Those who had known the vanished people stated that it was only those they had deemed Christian fanatics and innocent children who had been taken away.

A brewery worker was known to have said: "Yes! Hans Olsen is gone now, and probably it is what he used to preach about here. He always said Jesus was to come and fetch him!"

"Yes," replied another, "We had someone like that, and he's gone, too. Now I suppose the authorities will have to forbid all religion so such a thing can't happen again. "

"Ah, no!" exclaimed a third. "It will never occur again. Doubtless these Christians were right, for they had a premonition about it. If we'd only listened to them perhaps it would have been better for us than to have to live in this hell and chaos that is breaking over us now, and will probably get worse."

"So you believed in them?" - someone else added. "Then you ought to have gone with them when they went."

"I wish I had been able to do that," answered the other, as he turned to go on his way. One of the listeners called after him:

"You should be hanged, both you and all other people who concern themselves with this feebleminded Christianity!"

The following day, the newspapers could not give any explanation of the mystery, which remained obstinately unsolved, while from every country in the world reports continued to pour into news centers. From missionary stations it was reported that many Christian people had disappeared and that only a small number of Christians were left behind.

At the meeting called by the bishop quite a number of priests and clergymen proved to be present, although many of their erstwhile colleagues had also been carried away. A nervous and dismal atmosphere prevailed throughout the assembled people. A report on the meeting stated that many were very unhappy, but there was no doubt in anyone's mind that what had happened was the "rapture of the Christian Church, or, as some people had called the forthcoming event, "The Fetching of the Bride of Christ."

Some clergymen at the meeting confessed that in spite of their theological training and studies of the Bible, they had never believed it would happen in this way. Neither had they ever heard of regeneration. One young clergyman stated:

"I have never been taught in such a way. The professors didn't speak of the possibility of such a thing happening in these days!"

There was a tendency to discussion, but 'minds were too disturbed for such talk to be matter of fact. This was commented upon by a journalist reporting on the meeting. Subsequently, a report based on the findings of the meeting was drawn up, which the police proposed to lay before the public to test their opinion. Most of those participating at the meeting were agreed on the contents, which were presented in these terms:

"What has happened as a predicted Biblical event, the so-called "Rapture of the Christian Church, or, "Return of Christ for His Bride," which meant that Christ had taken His people from the earth. At present this was all that could be said."

The police proved uneasy about presenting such a statement to the public, thinking it was the product of a nervous and hysterical imagination. Also, they felt that the matter was of so far-reaching a nature that it should be dealt with at Government level. If, in fact, it proved to have anything to do with the Christian religion, perhaps, all churches and religious houses ought to be closed until a better view of events had been obtained and the affair clarified. This being an international problem, perhaps there should be a common attitude to the affair. Perhaps the U.N. would take charge and examine the problem thoroughly.

Among the Christians, the atmosphere seemed to be very pressing and heavy. On the first Sunday after the disappearance of the people all churches and meeting places were full to capacity. In some churches there was no minister, and many of the erstwhile members were reported to have disappeared. In others there was a sprinkling of believing people left, but in addition there was an enormous stream of outsiders who had, in most cases, met with "the great accident," as they termed it.

People were desirous of hearing God's word, but now it was obscured. Someone tried to read from the Bible, but after a brief attempt he said: "I don't understand anything." The Bible was handed to another, but he said, "I can't read it!" Other people wept. The majority seemed to be united about Christianity being the direct cause of this tragic event, and they had thought they could obtain a possible explanation of this thing at Christian places of worship. Many had come to seek God's help. They were profoundly unhappy.

At most meetings there was total confusion. At one, a man stood with clenched fists and cried to the clergyman: "It's your fault that so many of us have been left! You never told us that Jesus was to return to fetch His people, and still less about having a pure heart, being filled with the Holy Ghost and having everything straight with God and our fellow men! I know what has held me back! Small things, yes, small things, but... but, God help me!"

"Be silent!" said the clergyman. He considered he had done his duty.

Thus it went on, one person blaming another, intermingled with roaring and crying. They were knocking, but the door was closed!

The state of growing panic can hardly be described. People realized that a terrible time was to come. All hope had gone. The gate was irrevocably closed. They knocked and cried - all those who had been content with empty Christian words. Some had professed Christianity for the sake of fellowship; others only because they had had different tasks as choir members and in the music section. Still they had been without regeneration, without the adoption of Sons, and by that the right also of the inheritance of God given through Jesus Christ. Indeed, for many the life they had led as members of church congregations was no different from taking part in any section of society's activities; a hobby to help leisure time go faster. But now they all knocked at the door crying, "My Lord! My Lord, open the door to me!"

In addition to all this, horrible rumors began to circulate that the Third World War was liable to break out at any moment. Diplomatic relations between East and West were broken off, Terror grew.

Concerning the taking of Christ's Church from the earth and what to do about Christian people, it took the authorities short time to reach a decision. From the Eastern states an edict was issued to the effect that the communist states now were at the head of everything, and that all Christian activity and meetings now were forbidden by law. This was accompanied by threats of the death penalty, and the mention of the name of Jesus Christ was also forbidden. Countries were to be completely purged of Christian literature. With the Bible uppermost everything was to be burnt. To have anything which in any way related to the Christian religion meant death to the owner.

In the Western States it took a somewhat longer time before such prohibitions were brought into force. But the Godless members of the people, both among the authorities and the common people, were shocked over what had happened and demanded that something drastic should be done. The majority won, and since Christianity was stated to be the cause of the accidents to the community, the result was in no doubt.

Thus the most terrible time in the history of mankind began. Á great number of the Christian people left went on crying to God, refusing to obey the prohibitions. They were promptly arrested and examined under Gestapo conditions. "If you want to save your life, curse and deny Jesus Christ!" was the appalling statement.

In spite of this horror, thousands of people stood firm, and the wholesale murdering which followed was indescribable. Many victims were tormented until they died. There was no true law and order any more: SATAN WAS LET LOOSE. WOE TO THE WORLD, AND THEY WHO LIVE ON IT!

Several people yielded during this terrible pressure: They had no place to which they could flee, and the Scripture was being fulfilled, that "the whole earth is in the mercy of the wicked one." All countries were now united in their opinion about the extermination of Christians and Christianity. The prince of this world had now taken his power. Children betrayed their parents to their deaths.

Thus was fulfilled that which is written in the Gospel of Luke, Chapter 21:16, "AND THEY SHALL BE BETRAYED BOTH BY PARENTS AND BRETHERN AND KINSFOLKS AND FRIENDS; AND SOME OF YOU SHALL THEY CAUSE TO BE PUT TO DEATH... AND YE SHALL BE HATED OF ALL MEN FOR MY NAME'S SAKE."

Such a situation would appear impossible to describe, but God has given us knowledge of the whole thing in the Book of Revelation. The cry of the unhappy people left on the earth was: "Lord! Make these days shorter!"

My dear friend! You ought not to risk being left when Jesus comes to fetch His people, but you can know what to do about it. Go to God in prayer and ask for light and grace. Today there is time. Today you can be sealed as the property of Jesus Christ, and will be numbered among His people when He returns to fetch them.

For other new age scripts and prophecies write to the above address.

The Responsibility of Ones in High Places

--Soran

Soran Speaking -

Beloved Ones -- This day let us consider the great responsibility of the ones which sit in "high" places -- These are responsible for the conduct of themself - as well as the ones over which they preside ---

174

Now it is given unto thine people to call themself free - "A FREE PEOPLE" -- Wherein have they been free? ----

Wherein have they free speech?

- freedom of action?

I say they know <u>not</u> freedom! -- They but <u>think</u> themself free -- While they are bound by flesh / by the law of gravity (?) - by the attraction of the Moon - the <u>tides</u> - by mans opinion - his actions - and for the most part their own legirons! ---

Yea - I say unto <u>them</u> - they know not freedom -- Yet - they shall endure greater bondage ere they know the freedom of which I speak ---

They have accumulated many legirons - many - many laws have they made for themself - which they shall be responsible for -- They have not obeyed the Law which wast given unto them from the beginning -- They have transgressed the first Law -- This is the pity -- While they revile against the ones which transgress the law which they are wont to make and enforce - <u>they</u> have transgressed ALL the "Commandments" given unto them! ---

I say unto them: "Be ye responsible for that which ye set into motion - and be ye without blemish"-- Be ye spotless of character - - Let thine Light so shine that ALL might honor thee - and know that thou art of good character -- Be ye not tainted with / or by the wonton of fornication - the fornication which is given into them in high places of thine society ---

Be ye clean of hands - and be ye pure of thought-- Let not thine hard be swift to pull down the "Standard of the Crown and the Cross" - shall it not be thine deliverance? -- Be ye swift to uphold law and justice - the LAW of which I speak ---

For it is the LAW OF JUSTICE - and no man is to be excluded - or exempt - for their position or Earthly stature ---

I say - because of position in "high places" they shall not be exempt -- These shall be the beacon lights - These shall be the pillars of Government -- These shall walk as ones sober - as ones justified -- And they shall be beyond reproach -- For I say - they shall serve well their fellow men - their Brethren - impartially and without malice or prejudice ---

I say these shall be given a part within the Government of the Earth - and therein shall be placed the ones which shall set straight that which hast been made crooked -- So be it the hypocrites shall be removed into a corner - and they shall learn well their lesson -- For this shall they be given a lesser part -- It is said "Pity is the one which betrays himself / or his trust" So it is ---

I come that ye might know that which is designed - that which shall come to pass -- Yet each and every one shall be responsible for his part within the "NEW ORDER" -- I say none shall shirk his responsibility -- So be it that I have spoken unto thee -- Pass not the "Word" until thou hast considered well thine own responsibility!

I AM Soran

(This is given at a time when the actions of high ranking politicians are being questioned)

176

The Coming Planned Aggression

The Chinese have planned an invasion using a very peculiar type of biological agent. They will infiltrate through what they estimate is their weakest enemy. In this case, they will begin what we can call the invasion of the Western Hemisphere through the uppermost area – Canada. Key agents will locate themselves in major cities located near the East Coast, such as Montreal and Quebec; at the same time, the northeastern cities, of the United States will be included, as far south as Washington, D.C.

This systematic plan will bring the destruction of people by the millions. These germs will be released through the water supply; as planned, within a twenty-four hour period, most of the population in these affected areas would be destroyed. The Chinese do not expect that they would have to worry about the population in surrounding areas, because panic would take care of the rest.

They are not particularly worried about the Midwest, since they consider that that area is not powerful and unable to defend itself. On the West Coast, however, they plan on doing the same thing they will do on the East Coast.

They figure on getting very little resistance from Canada, since it is a very weak country, militarily as well as govermentally. The reason they need to do this within an eighteen month period is that they realize that negotiations between the United States, Russia and Canada are getting far too close…They fear this. They figure that the time is right now to do this thing.

Many of their envoys, many of their diplomatic missions have brought much into their country, since they cannot be stopped, searched or seized. Some of the things they have developed are very powerful, and yet they could be carried in very small containers.

We are allowing this to happen, it will happen, but we won't allow it to happen exactly as they plan. True, much of Canada will be destroyed, as far as human beings are concerned. True, the upper portion of the United States, especially New York, Washington, D.C., New Jersey-- those areas right along the coast-- will be pretty much destroyed, as far as population is concerned.

Yet, as the Chinese move in closer to the magnetic portions of the United States, such as Ohio and Arkansas -- especially these two areas, these two centers -- they will not be able to advance, because there are people being prepared -- people that are not afraid of this, people that are able to overcome this, because they are one with God: they have already taken their bodies into a union with the Higher Force. They will drink, but it will not destroy them. For instance, your scriptures even tell you that they will drink deadly things and will not die. (This is only if a person has that Christ mind.)

We wish you to know this, that you must delay it. In other words, spirit force does not cancel things. We try to impregnate your minds, that you might learn to rule right, that you might learn how to govern. You realize that over every town, over every city, over every nation, over every planet there are spirit beings of varying degrees who govern those planets, those cities, those towns. You also must realize that they can be influenced, they can be helped by your thoughts.

If the governing forces of a certain city are having trouble controling that city, we guide individuals who are embodied to go to that city; since thy are human beings, they move among the people of that city to change the vibrations of those people, to bring about the peace which they have within themselves. In other words, everything moves from spirit; as a result, the earthly condition is changed.

Yet you must realize that you are spirit beings in a temple. Many lifetimes have prepared you for this day, for this New Age: You are that Age. You have come here to Study. Some of you have come here to learn more of your psychic abilities. Some of you have come here to learn more of Governmental things. Some of you have come here merely to enhance your own being. Yet those with whom you will come into contact with later might be taught, ever your offspring.

Now you know the basic plan. The chinese will think they have conquered. As their armies move in, they will come by boat, they will come down through Canada, moving, then, through the United States. Then they will see a people prepared for them. They will die in fear, because they will see you as you really are, not in your physical form, but as you really are. Then they will die in fear, and they will be stopped.

The plan is for eighteen months. Yet, if you do the things you are to do, if you write to these places where you know to write, if you tell them of the coming aggession, then this could be held in abeyance. We will do certain things to hamper them. We will do certain things to limit their technology. We control these things, we control their thoughts. We will not allow it to happen until the time

179

is right. So do not fear for your country. But, this is all dependent on your willingness to follow instruction, to do that which you know to do.

Do not be lethargic in your own attitude, but persevere. For this is a school, this earth – a school to teach you how to rule and to reign; If you learn at the present time, then, during the coming years, it will be much easier for you, as well as for other people who depend upon you...

Question: What are we to do about this water pollution? Will boiling it help?

Answer: The agents that they have developed cannot be stopped by the filtaration methods that you now use. Also, they cannot be smelled or tasted; that is why gross devastation will be brought upon Canada and the United States. People will not be award; because of this, they will dring and die within twenty four hours; once they have tasted it, it will be too late.

The mass hysteria and the mass confusion will utterly bring death to while cities. We have tried to help people. We have blacked out the lights of several cities, for instance, New York City, to show people that they need to be more serious, they do not need more dollars, luxurious homes and large cars. They need to get within themselves, and realize the purpose of life, and begin to love one another, and begin to seek our guidance and cease arguing.

Question: Well, there's nothing that can be done about it, then, I suppose, except to pray, learn and help.

Answer: Yes, this avails much more than you realize. You must realize that your vibrations are not confined to this room. You must start to take stock of yourselves. It is not good for a person to think more highly of himself than he ought, nor is it good for him to think more lowly of himself than he ought. Rather, seek to know yourself, know the being that dwells within you, learn to command, learn to take dominion over things. We guide you, we show you when to do things, and how to do things, so that you can be ready for that day when mankind will need your direction and leadership. So do not fear: All things are in our hands, all things are worked out for the good of mankind....

I am not of the Masters around you. I am from a star which is governing this planet. I am an energy force....

NOTE: This message was received in class during July, 1973, by one of our channels, T. B.

A message to students and friends of THE ASSOCIATION OF SANANDA AND SANAT KUMARA:

After receiving in the mail, "THE COMING PLANNED AGGRESSION", which you have just read, Sister Thedra asked Sananda, "Does this come from a valid source?"

Sananda's answer: "Yes, and it is so that the plan is lain. Yet it shall be aborted by and thru the ones which know. I ask! Art thou one with the plan, ye which read?

Serious, they do not need more dollars, luxurious homes and large cars. They need to get within themselves, and realize the purpose of life, and begin to love one another, and begin to seek our guidance and cease arguing.

Question: Well, there's nothing that can be done about it, then, I suppose, except to pray, learn and help.

Answer: Yes, this avails much more than you realize. You must realize that your vibrations are not confined to this room. You must start to take stock of yourselves. It is not good for a person to think more highly of himself than he ought, nor is it good for him to think more lowly of himself than he ought. Rather, seek to know yourself, know the being that dwells within you, learn to command, learn to take dominion over things. We guide you, we show you when to do things, and how to do things, so that you can be ready for that day when mankind will need your direction and leadership. So do not fear: All things are in our hands, all things are worked out for the good of mankind....

I am not of the Masters around you. I am from a star which is governing this planet. I am an energy force....

NOTE: This message was received in class during July, 1973, by one of our channels, T. B.

A message to students and friends of THE ASSOCIATION OF SANANDA AND SANAT KUMARA:

After receiving in the mail, "THE COMING PLANNED AGGRESSION", which you have just read, Sister Thedra asked Sananda, "Does this come from a valid source?"

Sananda's answer: "Yes, and it is so that the plan is lain. Yet it shall be aborted by and thru the ones which know. I ask! Art thou one with the plan, ye which read?

Traitors in High Places

Beloved; - Now it is said and rightly so, that there are "None so sad as he which betrays himself, or his trust"; yet thou hast seen not the last of it, for I say that there are ones which doth sit in high places, which have the part of betraying their trust; for I say: They have sold the freedom of their fellow countrymen for a "pence" - I say, "FOR A PENCE". Now let it be recorded here in this Script, that there are many true and just within the high places; yet this is as it should be! and they are not to be overlooked; for I say: Were it not for them, thy nation would no longer be a Nation of people, white or black; neither brown or yellow; neither red, for it should be destroyed completely! I say, were it not for the just and true ones.

Yet I say. There are ones which doth sit in high places which have sold their worth; they have given unto the Dragon great praise; and glorified him! I say: They have spoken with a double tongue - forked with three prongs, as it were. For I say, they speak in riddles that the people know NOT that which they say. They ask of thee the sweat of thy brow, and the labor of thy hands - FOR WHAT? I say, they have said this, and that, and thou hast forgotten what hast been said, for they talk so loud and long, thou cannot hear them, - for I say, the ones which have tried, cannot follow their places - I say their places. I say, they are as actors which go from scene unto scene, using many parts, which are not convincing which are not as the script; they do not follow the script, shall we say - not in THEIR play - their game!

I say, they are playing a losing game, these false ones. I say unto thee: They are FALSE, and they are not at peace with themself! I say too, that they - the false ones, shall find one on which to place his blame, for he shall be as one undefended and unprotected by the world of men. Now let Me say it thusly: - "ONE" shall bear the burden of many traitors, for there are more than ye care to know! Not that that ye shall not know them, for I say, they shall be exposed, - for have I not said that justice shall reign supreme? and all things shall be weighed and balanced? Have I not said that there are none so sad as the one which betrays himself or his trust? It is SO! Yet the fools that they are, heed not the law - yet they shall be caught up short of their course. Let it suffice that, each unto his own, and each shall receive as he is prepared.

And I say: Great is the law, and swift doth it deal out JUSTICE! Let not thy heart be troubled, for I say, that there are ones prepared for that which shall be done, and not one of thy Sibors shall be caught off guard! Too, has it not been said that this is MY LAND, MY COUNTRY - have I not founded it? Have I not guarded it? Yet there shall be trying times; it shall be purged, cleansed and purified, and I shall set up My Banner, and NOTHING shall prevail against it! I have spoken fearlessly and justly. I say, I shall point them out ONE by ONE! and ye shall know them.

I AM thy Sibor, Sananda

Recorded by Sister Thedra

Traitors Shall Be Traitors Still

Mine Beloved Children; - The hour swiftly approaches when the days shall grow colder and the nights shall be longer, and the willful shall be as the wonton still - the traitors shall be traitors still for the traitors shall remain traitors; yet the loyalist shall remain. Now I say unto thee: The time of great suffering is come and great sorrow is upon them; and they shall cry out for Mercy, and they shall find that they have betrayed themself, for I say: They have been warned again and again. They shall look well unto the help which is proffered them; yet I say: They have turned their face from Me, and they have given unto Me "Gall for water!"

I say: They have given unto Me "gall for water", for I have stood by, asking of them naught, save that they prepare themself for this day. Yet they have not needed Mine Words; they have cast lots for Mine garments, while they have crucified Me. I say: They do put the swaddling clothes before the babe; I am come that they know the difference,- that they might be up and about their preparation; for this is the cry going forth this day: "Prepare! Prepare!"

Prepare for what? they ask! I say: For the accounting, for the balancing; for it is now come when the accounting shall be made, and the balancing established. So be it that they have made a mockery of Mine Word and ridiculed Me, and I say, they have made images of Me, and bowed down before them, saying their foolish rigamaroles, and knowing NOT that by them they are bound. Let it pass and be no more; let it pass and be finished, for I am come that they have Light.

So be it I Am the Light, the Truth and the Way, for I Am the Lord thy God.

Sananda

Recorded by Sister Thedra of the Emerald Cross

To the Ones in High Places

Sanat Kumara speaking; - Ye shall now give unto them this Word, and it shall go out unto all which are of a mind to learn.

I say unto them, that it is now come when they shall be as ones which have burned the midnite oil, and they have wasted their substance for they have sown unto the wind; they have been as the ones which have gathered into themself tares and thistles. I say: They have wasted their substance, and they have not taken thot or the Father which has given unto them being. Now I say unto them, they have given unto themself credit for being wise, when they have been the greatest of fools - I say, they have been fools.

Now I say unto them which sit in high places, that there are none so foolish as the one which thinks himself wise, and none so sad as he which betrays himself or his trust. For it is now come when the traitors shall be brot to account for his foolishness, and he shall be as one cast out. I say he shall be as one cast out, for he has not reckoned with the law; he has not given credit where credit is due; he has not been unto himself true - nor has he been unto his trust true. He has been unto himself traitor; he has bartered in human sacrifice; he has been as one which has upon his hand the blood of the saints, the blood of his children, and the blood of his brother; I

186

say, he has even sacrificed his father and mother that he be given the privilege of serving the one cast down - the dragon. I say, he shall come to know that which has held him bound hand and foot to be the dragon, which has gone the long way to bind him.

Now I say unto thee which have a mind to learn, that there are none so sad as the one which betrays his trust, for he shall suffer the consequences, and he shall be as one cast out.

For the first time I say unto them which betray themself, that they shall go unto a place which is prepared for them, wherein they shall begin at the beginning, they shall have their memory blanked from them, and they shall know not that which they now boast of, - the knowledge of which they boast shall be as naught, and all their opinions shall go as the chaff before the wind.

I speak unto them which are so minded to serve the forces of darkness. And when ye have given of thyself that ye may be glorified, and thy appetites satisfied, ye shall be as ones which have given of thy strength and of thyself that thy brother may suffer that which is unbearable; and I say, woe unto any man which gives unto his brother the bitter cup. Such is My word unto thee, and ye shall study well these My Words, for ye shall have cause to remember them.

I am come that they may be delivered up, which have a mind unto peace, and them which have a mind unto learning; I shall give unto then wisdom and peace which no man shall take from them; and I am of the mind to give unto them as I have received of the Father. Such is My inheritance that I am One with the Father, and all the Father has is Mine to give, for He has endowed unto me all that He is and all that He has. And for this do I say: Be ye as one prepared for to receive Me and of Me, for inasmuch as ye do receive Me, ye shall receive the Father, and as ye receive Him and of Him, so shall ye receive thy Godhood. Amen and Selah.

I AM thy Older Brother, Sanat Kumara

Recorded by Sister Thedra

Traitors

Behold the Lord thy God; - I speak unto thee in tongues, the tongue of thine which thou hast comprehension of; for this have I said unto thee: Be ye or a mind to learn of Me, for I shall go the last mile that ye might be enlightened of Me. I tell thee of a surety that thine enlightenment cometh not of man's opinion - his ideas or his books, for he is the one which has accumulated his works thru the ages, and by the power of the Word which hast gone out from the Inner Temple hast he been enlightened. He hast not been enlightened thru the opinions of men; their legirons have held them fast. While I say: We have sent messengers unto them without number, they have forgotten the message.

While they have tomes unto them, about them, and lauded their praise - sung their hymns unto them; yet they have slaughtered / crucified / martyred them, and made of them a thing of ridicule - while they have spat upon the hand of them which would have led them out of bondage. I say they are the traitors; they betray themself, for they have turned a deaf ear unto Mine "WORD"; they have chosen their own way, and hard indeed is the way of the traitor. So be it I shall say more of them, and ye shall give it unto them.

188

So be it I AM Sananda

Hail! Hail Unto the Victor!

Beloved Ones; - This day I speak unto thee of great and glorious things. Yet too I say, that there shall be the tears which flow from the eyes of the willful; from the ones which stand by and see the changes as they do take place. For it shall come to pass that there shall be great sorrow, for and because of the wanton and willful ones. For this have We thine Older Brothers said unto thee: Put on the whole Armor of God, and ye shall stand firm as the rock, and ye shall not be as the traitors; ye shall be as ones which have thine hand in Mine, and I shall lead thee and direct thee. Let it be said that: "There shall be tears, yea, bitter tears!" yet there shall be great joy! Yea, greater joy than man hast known; for I know the joy of the Victor, the one which attains unto his freedom. Let it be said, that the joy which is ours shall be thine, for it is now come when ye shall step forth and know that thou art Sons of God; that thou hast not been unto thineself traitor. Ye shall overcome; ye shall be the Victor I say: "Hail! Hail unto the Victor! Welcome home!"

I am the One which hast come that ye might attain thine victory. So shall it be.

I AM Sananda

Recorded by Sister Thedra

The Aggressor (War Mongers)

This day I would say unto thee; - Hold high Mine Lamp, and give unto them this Word as it is given unto thee. It is now time for a great revelation of the reality which shall bring unto then great light; for it is time that they mow wherein they are staid. I say, they shall come to know that which is hidden from them; for this do I speak out this day.

Now it is given unto them to deny Me - Mine existence - Mine teaching, and they dare defy the law - the law which has been given unto them from the beginning; the law which says: "Love ye one another - thou shall not kill - love thine neighbor as thineself" - these things have they ignored! these things they do not! And I say unto them: Be ye as ones which fan the coals for thine own feet, for ye shall walk upon them; ye shall drink of the poison cup which thou hast prepared for thine brother - enemy, sayest thou! I ask of thee: Art thou friend when thou prepare a lair for thine brother, what is this, friend or foe? Wherein is there justice and mercy amongst them? I say, they are traitors and they shall be dealt with justly. So be it I am not the judge, yet I know the law.

Now I say unto thee, ye which have a mind to follow where I lead thee: Pray for them - love them; yet ye shall be no part of their foolishness, their hypocrisy, for they make a mockery of that which they call righteousness - they are not righteous! they are as the traitors, and worse than infidels; they are hypocrites - they are as a stench unto Me, for I know them for that which they are. They are not the CHRISTians - the loyalists - the godly saints they profess to be. I say, they stand with blood stained hands, and they shall be held accountable unto the law. So be it I have spoken out against them; so be it I shall set Mine hand against them, and they shall be put to the end; there shall be an end to the aggressor - the aggression, - be it where it may, it shall end. So let it be according unto the Will of the Father which hast sent Me, for I am come that there be Light. So let it be.

I AM Sananda

Recorded by Sister Thedra

I Did Say: I Shall Return

Behold - I Am Come! The One which hast awaited this day, when I might walk among them which hast kept their covenant with Me. I say unto them: I am come that Mine Part might be fulfilled; I say unto them: I come that ye might go where I go.

Now, it is come when I have returned unto thee for the purpose of fulfilling Mine Promise - Mine Covenant, that it might be finished THIS DAY. Never wast it finished, for I did say: "I shall return unto thee that where I go ye might go also" - So let it be.

For this do I say unto thee: "Be ye about thine preparation that it might be so". So let it be as the Father hast Willed it. I come that His Will be done in Me - thru Me, and by Me, this day - So let it be. I say unto thee: Let it be done! for I am come unto thee that it be done; as He hast sent me for that purpose. Call unto then which hast ears to hear, and say unto them as I would say; that "He is come, that where He goes ye might go also". So let them hear that which I say this day,- be it the Truth and the Light by which they shall come.

I give unto thee of Mineself that they might come to know Me. So be it they that have ears to hear, shall know Mine Voice and respond unto it.

191

Let thine Light so shine that they MIGHT FOLLOW IT.

So be it I AM the Lord thy God

Sananda

Recorded by Sister Thedra of the Emerald Cross

The Lord God vs The Magician

Beloved Ones; - There is a Plan - a time of fulfillment, and the joy of that fulfillment no man knows. So be it that I see the joy of its completion, for I see it as done. And the time swiftly approaches when it shall be given unto thee to see as I see; so be ye not anxious for that which is yet to come. Wait upon Me, the Lord thy God; give unto Me credit for knowing that which I say unto thee; fear not for that which thou hast not yet seen - that which is to be. Be ye blest this day, and give unto thineself Peace and Poise. Seek not the fortune of the magicians, for they are not of Mine Flock, for I give unto thee that which is sufficient unto thine salvation.

I say: There are magicians which give unto them that which they seek - yet it is not the ultimate; it is not that which bringeth into them eternal freedom. I am come that thine bondage be ended that thine ETERNAL FREEDOM be thine THIS DAY. So be it I say: "Follow ye Me"; yet they weary of Mine Sayings, and they turn unto the magicians, that they might see his miracles! that they might be given the miracles of flesh - the signs and wonders which doth astound them. So be it that they are astounded by that which he does; for this do they follow him - the wonder-maker - the magician.

I say: "I come not to astound them, neither to bewilder them - I come that they might come into the FULLNESS of their inheritance". So be it I give unto them that which is sufficient unto their salvation; yet they have as yet not given unto ME credit for being that which I AM.

I say unto them which ask of Me: "Come! follow ye Me and I shall counsel thee, and I shall lead thee out of bondage FOREVER". So let it BE.

For I come NOT preaching a strange or NEW DOCTRINE; I simply give unto thee the Law which is as of old, - that which shall be unto thee thine passport into the place wherein I AM. I ask of thee nothing save obedience unto these, and therein is thine own freedom. So be ye as one self-responsible; I am come that it be SO.

I AM Sananda

Recorded by Sister Thedra of the Emerald Cross

The Magical Rites

Beloved Ones; - There is but One God, One Lord God, One Mighty and High Council - "ONE", and none other shall ye serve, for I say unto thee: There are ones which set up their own altars, and they build great and wonderous temples unto their strange and powerful gods, which hold them bound. They give unto these "gods" the power to hold them, for they pay homage unto them; they perform magical rites unto them; they ask of them favors - signs and wonders - knowing not that by these they are bound unto their "strange gods". They have not learned that they bind themself into these strange and

193

false gods. They are wont to give unto Me credit for being that which I AM, yet they give unto these the power to deceive then by their magical rites; they have NOT learned that they alone give unto these the power to hold them within their grasp.

These are the ones which seek signs and wonders, knowing not that these are the tools with which the magician can bind them. I say: Be ye alert; hold high Mine Lamp - that which I have given unto thee. Walk ye not with them which would MISLEAD, for they but give unto thee the bitter cup. I say: Be ye as ones blest to hear that which I say unto thee, and I shall be unto thee sufficient unto the day. Rest not on thine "Laurels for there is yet greater things in store for thee. Be ye as ones alert, - let no man trip thee up, for it is now come when the dragon shall be brot out into the open, and he shall be exposed for that which he is!

I say: "Ye shall know him for that which he is". He shall have no power over thee, while thou art with Me, for I have said unto thee: "I am thine shield and thine buckler", so it is; IT IS SO, for I am not a traitor! Yet I say unto thee: Turn not thine face from Me; keep thine eyes fixed upon the Way in which I lead thee, for I shall lead thee aright. Fall not unto "The Tempter", for he shall do a work which is designed to tempt all men to follow him.

Be ye as ones forewarned of his "Magic"; believe him not, for he is a LIAR, and the truth is not within him. I come that ye know the true from the false.

I AM Sananda

Recorded by Sister Thedra of the Emerald Cross

Rescue from the Oppressor

Mine Children; - Ye shall partake of Mine banquet table; ye shall feast and be filled to capacity; ye shall be satisfied, and no more shall ye hunger - I say, NO MORE shall ye hunger, for I shall satisfy thine hunger, and thine longing shall be no more. I say unto thee: "Thine longing shall be satisfied, and no more shall ye go into bondage - darkness".

Mine Children; - I have sent Mine emissaries unto thee - without number have they come, and they have been oppressed, and they have been martyred for thine sake, for the love which they bore. Yet I say: It is now time that they be finished, that they be brot out from amongst the oppressors; and no longer shall they bear the burdens of the laggards - the oppressors. I say they shall complete their mission, and return unto their abiding place wherein they shall be free from all bondage - wherein they shall know no sorrow or oppression. I say: Them which have given their all selflessly, shall partake of Mine board, and they shall have no wants, no fear, no sorrow. So shall it be a glad day when they return unto Me, unscathed, unharmed, purified and justified.

To the Oppressor

I speak unto them which know not that this day is come, when I shall bring out Mine "Flock" from among the multitude which hast oppressed them. Be ye alert, and know that the Law of Justice shall reign supreme, and there shall be justice for all - according unto his works. I say: Ye shall be judged with righteous judgment, and it shall be meted out according to the law of justice, which is exacting.

Be ye not so foolish as to <u>think</u> ye escape the law; I say, ye shall be into thine own self true, and unto thine trust true. Be ye mindful of Mine Words, and Mine servants which I have sent that ye might have light. I say, ye shall be blest according unto thine works, and ye shall bless others as ye would be blest. I speak out this day that ye might come to know that I AM COME, come that there be Light. So let it be.

I AM the Lord thy God, Sananda

Recorded by Sister Thedra

I Am Come That It Cease

This day, let it be understood that the way has been made clear that ye might return unto thine rightful estate - thine abiding place. It is given unto Me to make strait the way; and for this am I called the "WAY SHOWER"; for this do I say: "Follow ye Me, that where I go ye might go also". And it shall be for thine own enlightenment that I give unto thee this Word; - that there are a great many which have come with Me that the way be prepared before thee. It is given unto US, the HOST, to see that which goes on, and that which is being done; yet we stand by in readiness, to be unto thee the hand and foot - so swift that no man could follow in its flight. The time is come when naught shall stay US; for the time is come when great stress is upon the land, and the people thereof has within their hand the power to get into motion that which could destroy the Earth, and at no time shall we allow that. For this it is given unto us the power and the authority to stop that which has been brot about by their own willfulness and wanton. I say: The time is come when we shall interfere with the plan of men!!

196

For they have gone so far as to give unto the EARTH the bitter cup, which shall be unto Her her destruction without Our help. So shall it be assured Her, that she shall not perish at the hands of the dragon!!

I have set Mine Hand against them, and they shall know that it is SO - so shall it BE.

While they dare call themself "Civilized and Christian", I say: They have not known the meaning of ETHIC - they are not of Mine fold. So be it that I am about Mine Father's business and I fear not; and I say unto them: "Make way! for I am at the helm". And I pass, and they shall stand in awe, and know that I have passed. So be it I shall pass them by, and they shall cry out for assistance, and I shall not hear their cry, - for they have set their foot against Me and betrayed themselves. So be it I have spoken out against the war mongers, and the ones which set brother against brother; and son against father, mother against daughter, and sister against brother.

I say: I speak out against them which set one against the other, that they might set their foot upon their necks. Let it be said, that it shall cease.

"Let it cease!' is the Word which hast gone out of Mine mouth, and it shall not return unto Me void. So be it I am come that IT CEASE!

I AM the Lord thy God, Sananda

Recorded by Sister Thedra

197

Made in the USA
Columbia, SC
14 February 2021